Play to Win
Rugby League Heroes

Maurice Bamford

London League Publications Ltd

Play to Win
Rugby League Heroes

© Copyright Maurice Bamford.
Foreword © Danny Lockwood.
Introduction © Ray French.
The moral right of Maurice Bamford to be identified as the author has been asserted.

Cover design © Stephen McCarthy. Photographs © copyright as credited to the photographer or provider of the photograph.

Front and back cover photos: Front: Maurice Bamford (photo: Sig Kasatkin – RLphotos.com); Back: Great Britain players build support before playing New Zealand in 1985. Maurice Bamford was the Great Britain coach (photo: Andrew Cudbertson).

A CIP catalogue record for this book is available from the British Library.

First published in Great Britain in July 2005 by:
London League Publications Ltd, P.O. Box 10441, London E14 8WR

ISBN: 1-903659-21-3

Cover design by: Stephen McCarthy Graphic Design
                                   46, Clarence Road, London N15 5BB

Layout: Peter Lush

Printed and bound by: Biddles Ltd
                                   King's Lynn, Great Britain

This book is dedicated to Rita, my long-time wife and mate, and to Harry Jepson (Leeds) and Jeff Wine (Bramley), two of the finest chairmen I worked with during my coaching career.

Sponsored by *League Weekly*

Foreword

The sport of rugby league has been undergoing a quiet revolution in recent times. The glitzy professionalism of Super League has bred a new generation of soccer-style superstars, the growth of the summer game has brought a brand new audience of devotees, and across the land 'converts' to the sport are fuelling the game's development at hitherto undreamt of pace.

Yet rugby league remains a game whose very ethos is rooted in community and tradition. No heroes of today or tomorrow could ever eclipse the men of yesteryear; creatures, it often seemed, made of sterner, steelier stuff than we mere mortals. Their names and legends are inscribed indelibly in the annals of the clubs that spawned them, and whose colours they carried to glory, from Central Park to Headingley, to Wembley and across the seas to Auckland, Sydney and beyond.

One man in that rare position of being able to stand astride those bulwarks of the ancient and modern, to cast the eye of professional judgment on all of the qualities that makes a special rugby league player, is Maurice Bamford. Born and bred at the working class hearth place of the game, he was weaned on the rough and tumble of rugby league's raw education, graduated to coaching the biggest clubs in the British game, and indeed achieved the ultimate honour of leading his country out against the vaunted Australians. With that almost unrivalled experience within the game, Maurice is perfectly placed to bring those legends back to life.

Legend is a strange animal in itself. Stories of the great characters of yore appear to develop an organic personality of their own. The tales, like the men within them, become stronger, faster, and more blindingly artful in every re-telling. Our heroes' exploits capture new imaginations long after the deeds of derring-do have been soaked away in a muddy, bandage-strewn after-match bath at Station Road, or a crate of lukewarm brown ale has fuelled a clanking old team bus back across a frosty A62 on a bitter Pennine night.

As an accomplished raconteur and reporter of this, the greatest game, the relaying of the baton of rugby league's legends from one generation to another, can be well trusted to Maurice Bamford. Maurice has seen many of them as a boy, played with them as a youth and a man, and coached some on the greatest possible stages. As a thoroughbred rugby league professional, his judgments can be relied upon to marry the myth with the mortality, and to bring today's and tomorrow's legions of fans an entertaining and informative insight.

Danny Lockwood
Publisher, *League Weekly*

Introduction

Long after the match is over, few are able to remember the score. Advancing years cause even those who played in the game to forget who gave the final try-scoring pass or who made the last gasp match-saving tackle on the winger as he sped down the touchline. And yet league folk never fail to recall their teammates, the characters in the opposition line-up, and the friendships forged over a drink or two in the clubhouse following even the most ferocious of battles.

Maurice Bamford is one man who has occasion to recall more matches and with greater diversity then most, such has been his service to the game at all levels in both the professional and amateur sections of the XIII-a-side code. A rugby league devotee since his father first introduced him to the sport as a young lad, Maurice has never lost that youthful passion and innocent optimism whatever his circumstances and wherever he coached. Whether in charge of Great Britain and battling for national pride in a fiercely fought test series, inspiring league giants Wigan or Leeds to success, or nurturing blossoming talent in the amateur ranks at Stanningley, Lock Lane or Mirfield, he has never failed to realise that rugby league is about more than just gaining a result.

It is about companionship and spirit within the community; it is about ambition and setting personal goals, however limited, and, above all, it is about enjoyment on and off the pitch. No one is better equipped than Maurice to highlight the players he has coached or watched during his many years involvement in rugby league and no one is more capable of bringing to life the many characters he has met or able to recount their activities with such humour.

Statisticians can often reduce a sport to an endless list of records, tries and goals scored, trophies won or lost, and numbers of games played by individual personalities – a spine on which to hang the flesh of a game. In this book Maurice Bamford, with his sharp insight into rugby league and his deep knowledge of it, provides the flesh in abundance with humorous and serious tales of the heroes, villains and engaging characters he has been involved with throughout his colourful career.

Maurice's book is all about enjoyment and a respect for those men who play one of the hardest, and at times, most cruel of sports. And that enjoyment hits you on every page.

Ray French

Ray French played rugby union for England, and rugby league for Great Britain, St Helens and Widnes. He is BBC television's rugby league commentator, and one of the game's most distinguished journalists.

About the author

The railway viaduct that snakes across Kirkstall Road on the west side of the City of Leeds is constructed of Yorkshire granite. Its giant arches carry freight and passenger trains to and from the North of England, and as a kid the author stood on a banking and saw, at various times, Mallard and The Flying Scotsman hurtle past, not 10 yards away. Darnborough Street was my place of birth, in a one up, one down street house, only 100 yards from the viaduct, on the city side, in April 1936.

The Sacred Heart RC School in Burley Road was my place of learning from five years old until I was 14, when the 'senior boys' were moved up Cardigan Road to the annex of the Catholic sister church of Our Lady of Lourdes, which in turn, was about 400 yards from the Mecca of rugby league football, Headingley. Our only male teacher, Mr Joe Goodwin, was a gentleman of the old school. Seeing action as an infantryman in the Second World War, he returned home to teach at the school he left in 1939 and his first job was to introduce his pupils to the finer arts of the greatest game, rugby league.

I remember 'bunking off' school one Wednesday afternoon, to see the Leeds versus Australian tourists game in 1948, and as I crept behind the posts at the Kirkstall Lane end, to my horror I found myself stood next to none other than, Mr Joe Goodwin. Bending down to whisper in my ear, he said with a smile, "I won't tell if you don't, Maurice". That was the first time I ever saw 'The Little Master', Clive Churchill, at full-back for the tourists and as if it were yesterday, I recall him slicing through a good Leeds defence, like the proverbial knife through butter.

I signed as an amateur for Leeds and played in their successful junior team, but when the great Hull FC came for me in November 1953 I was swept away by the fabulous side that wore the black and white irregular hoops and played on that wonderful ground, The Boulevard. Transferred to Dewsbury in 1957, I had another very enjoyable six years at the old Crown Flatt ground until an injury to my hand and wrist put me out of the game from Christmas to the following August. I went to train with a good amateur side to get fit as they were training all through the close season. I stayed in amateur football for the remainder of my playing career, but did return to Dewsbury in 1972 as assistant coach after playing for Burton Sports and Stanningley in the Leeds and District League. The chief coach at Dewsbury was Tommy Smales, who left the club to coach his home town club, Featherstone Rovers and I was promoted to senior coach. My next professional job, after getting the sack at Dewsbury and returning to the amateur game to coach Stanningley, was as assistant coach to Arthur Keegan at Bramley, the first of my three stints as coach of that grand little club.

Peter Fox took over from Arthur Keegan and I went with Peter to Bradford Northern as his assistant and that started the roller-coaster ride in my coaching career. I proudly carry on my CV no fewer than 22 professional jobs as a rugby league coach, including Yorkshire County amateurs coach and the biggest of them all, the Great Britain rugby league coach from 1984 to 1986. Spells at Halifax, Huddersfield, Wigan, Leeds (twice), Workington Town, Dewsbury again, Blackpool Borough, York, Keighley, Prescot and Lancashire Lynx and a run in amateur coaching as diverse as Castleford Lock Lane in the National Conference Premier League, to Fifth Division Yorkshire League at Bailiff Bridge at 67 years old.

I have been married to my wife Rita since 1957, with one daughter, Jane, and two grandkids, Sarah (who must take after her grandma, as she earned a degree at Bradford University) and Daniel. Our Dan is currently out injured, but has played for Halifax and Batley at 19 years old. We live in Morley, the 'motorway town' and I continue my involvement in the game by writing match reports and a weekly column in *League Weekly*. So there it is - a brief introduction to the author.

The men in this book are a varied cross section of characters, not all internationals, but the type of man you would want with you if it came to 'Hey lads, hey', or the call of the old days: 'One in, all in'.

If I have missed anyone in my favourite players, I sincerely apologise, because if I had the space I would mention every single player that I played with and against and every player I had the honour to coach and work with in my many seasons in the finest, greatest game in the universe, rugby league football.

Maurice Bamford
July 2005

Maurice Bamford playing and coaching record

Playing: Hull FC and Dewsbury from 1953 to 1963.

Coaching:

Dewsbury	1972 - 1973 (Assistant)
Dewsbury	June 1974 - October 1974
Stanningley	1974 -1975
Bramley	1974-5 - 1976-7 (Assistant)
Dudley Hill	
Bradford Northern	June 1977 - February 1978 (Assistant)
Halifax	February 1978 - May 1980
Huddersfield	May 1980 - May 1981
Wigan	May 1981- May1982
Bramley	May 1982 - October 1983
Leeds	November 1983 – February 1985
GB	October 1984 – December 1986
Leeds	December 1986 – April 1988
Workington	July 1988 – December 1988
Dewsbury	December 1988 – December 1990
Bramley	April 1992 – September 1993
Blackpool Gladiators	
Greetland	
Prescot	February 1997 – May 1997
Mirfield	
York	
Keighley	
Lancs Lynx	Jun 2000 – Aug 2000
Castleford Lock Lane	
Bailiff Bridge	

Thank you

Maurice Bamford and London League Publications Ltd would like to thank the following for their help and support in publishing this book:
League Weekly for their sponsorship;
Danny Lockwood and Ray French for writing the foreword and introduction respectively;
Stephen McCarthy for designing the cover;
Robert Gate for providing most of the statistics and many photos;
David Williams and Sig Kasatkin of RLphotos.com, Andrew Cudbertson, Alex Service, Bernard Platt and *League Express* for providing photos;
Michael O'Hare for subediting;
The staff at Biddles Ltd for printing the book.

Photo credits:

All photos courtesy of Robert Gate, except as listed below or where credited by the photo:

RLphotos.com (David Williams & Sig Kasatkin): Dean Bell, Des Drummond, Andy Farrell, John Holmes, Brett Kenny, Wally Lewis, Keith Senior, David Ward.

Alex Service: Dick Huddart, Vince Karalius, Alex Murphy, Mick Sullivan, Tom van Vollenhoven, Cliff Watson.

Bernard Platt: Keiron Cunningham, Sean Long.

League Express: Dean Blankley.

Thanks to the following who supplied photos of themselves: Keith Mason snr, Ces Mountford, John Wolford.

Maurice Bamford supplied the photos of Stanningley ARLFC and Don Ellis.

Statistics

Australia appearances only include test matches, not World Cup or World Championship appearances. Other tour games are not included.

Great Britain appearances only include full international, World Cup or World Championship and test matches, not other tour games.

New Zealand appearances only include full international, World Cup or World Championship and test matches, not other tour games.

Contents

Eric Ashton MBE

If one could sit at a computer and design a centre threequarter, the resultant player would be Eric Ashton of Wigan. Well over six-feet tall, athletically built, a long strider with deceptive pace, a strong defender and brave, with a terrific footballer's brain, he was the perfect middle back, so good that he captained both his club and his country to magnificent victories during his long and successful career. Coming from the other side of the hill in Yorkshire, people like me thought that Eric was a Wigan lad, a born-and-bred pie-eater but, of course, he is a St Helens boy.

His wonderful long term partnership with the superb Billy Boston as Wigan and Great Britain's numbers two and three led to their two names being linked like Compton and Edrich, Hutton and Washbrook or in our game's terms, Shannon and McCue or Williams and Jenkins. The Boston and Ashton combination ruled the right-hand side of rugby league fields from Swinton to Sydney, Bradford to Brisbane and Widnes to Wollongong.

I am sure that Billy B would be the first to agree that Eric Ashton had a big influence on his middle career, because the centre's silky skills could open up any defences. As early as 1957, when he was 22 years-old, Eric won the first of his 26 Great Britain caps, when he was selected for the World Cup side to go to Australia. Captained by the great Alan Prescott of St Helens, this very strong squad came second to the home nation in the final league table. Eric was accompanied by his old mate Billy Boston.

The Wigan ace also gained a place on the successful 1958 tour and again in 1962 when he captained the Lions in a 2-1 Ashes test win. But it was the Challenge Cup that held a glittering romance for Eric Ashton. This magnificent player had the tremendous distinction of not only playing in six Wembley finals, but being captain of Wigan in all six, the club winning the superb silver cup three times during his reign.

In the 1960-61 cup run Wigan were drawn against a decent Leeds side at Headingley and I was at the game to witness a very tough, hard-fought draw. The replay was at Central Park the following Wednesday afternoon – there were no floodlights in those days - and a team mate of mine from Dewsbury, Jack Leonard, and I were working together on a building site and we decided to go. I have never seen as many people at a non-international match or a Wembley cup final; there must have been more than 40,000 crammed into Central Park and with the queues so long it was 15 minutes into the game before we got in. Wigan won the replay easily, 32-7, with Lewis Jones scoring a late try to spare the Leeds fans' blushes.

But it was not the ease of the Wigan win or their scoring of many brilliant tries in that replay that I remember. The incident that I recall vividly is of Eric Ashton, standing toe-to-toe, slugging it out with the big, tough farmer who played in the Leeds second-row, Jack Fairbank. Looking at the two, you would not have backed Eric Ashton with bad money. Eric was tall, but compared to big Jack he was a welterweight. Outweighed by at least two stones, Eric gave Jack a boxing lesson. No doubt if it had been in a telephone box, Fairbank would have smothered Eric, but out in the wide open spaces of Central Park, Eric danced and jabbed, danced and jabbed, each jab having the kick of a mule and each one finding the target. So hurt and frustrated was Jack, that in the end he lashed out with his boot, which put the whole 40 odd thousand spectators on Eric's side. Both were sent off, but Ashton was the undoubted champion boxer that day.

I mention in my piece on Billy Boston about the time almost the whole Dewsbury pack failed to stop him scoring in the corner at Central Park. Well, Eric Ashton was his centre that afternoon and I remember him picking up a kick through and aiming his lean-looking frame in my general direction. Cometh the hour, cometh the man and I don't think Eric saw me because I actually brought him down with a tackle that brought congratulations from my teammates. Full of confidence that comes with success, not long after, it was him and me again, but this time he saw me coming and, veering away, Eric suddenly straightened into the slight gap between me and a teammate, simultaneously hitting me with a hand-off that felt as if the stand had fallen on me, before sending Billy B over for another try.

A hero, hand-off or no hand-off, and one of many memories I keep of such great players and heroes such as Eric Ashton, MBE.

	App	Tries	Goals	Pts
Wigan	487+10	231	448	1,589
Lancashire	10	8	3	30
Great Britain	26	14	1	44

Puig-Aubert

The chain-smoking, ace goalkicker, with the 'matador' film star good looks, was the quintessential Frenchman. Short, stocky with those dusky Latin looks that had the ladies swooning from Paris to Perpignan. Puig-Aubert was a crowd pleaser. The French supporters adored him and whenever he nonchalantly strolled up from full-back to take a kick at goal they would begin their call to this master kicker, 'Pipette', 'Pipette', 'Pipette', his nickname. He was an immaculate kicker of a dead ball, an old-fashioned toe-ender and the first man I ever saw who teed up the ball on sawdust.

He was also the first, and last, player I ever saw who lit up a couple of cigarettes at half time while the coach was delivering his 'gee up'. I saw this in an international match at Headingley between England and France in the European Championship in 1950. Half time came, and in those days the players stayed out on the field for their lemons and, as the French team gathered around the coach, a helper on the French staff walked around to where Aubert was standing, lit up a fag and gave it to the French king-pin, who took a huge drag, inhaled and closed his eyes in ecstasy. Another cigarette was given to him and he lit it with the stub of the first which by now was almost done. In those days smoking was the adult thing to do. Humphrey Bogart did it, King George did it and Puig-Aubert did it.

Strangely, seeing this icon of sport, this national treasure of France, acting in a human way by smoking, just like my Dad, immediately made him a hero of mine, but he could also play a bit too. Aubert had a wonderful natural gift in that he was an extremely long and inch-perfect accurate kicker of a ball, both from the ground and out of his hands.

Going to a game then, one of the skills one looked forward to was a kicking dual between, usually, the full-backs. Now these duals were not merely kicking the ball as hard as you could, but controlled, intelligent kicking, putting the ball 40 yards downfield, with your forwards ringing the opposite fullback. As the ball was swerving and spiralling down to the catching player, your forwards would be telling him what they would do with him if he dropped it.

England's full-back at that time was Jimmy Ledgard, then of Leigh, and he could kick a long, long way, but not many could out-kick Aubert. His party piece was to put a couple of kicks short, bringing the other full-back upfield, then he would produce a mammoth punt that would go over the head of the advancing full-back and send him scurrying back, amid catcalls and cheers from the fans, towards his own line with the patient forwards in hot pursuit .

Another forté of Aubert's was the drop-goal, worth two points then. Again at Headingley I saw him feign to drop a goal with his right foot then, as three England forwards jumped up to block it, calmly switch to his left foot and land the drop-goal. Fantastic! Pipette would control a game with his kicking, not like today when coaches demand running the ball for five and kicking on the last, no, Pipette would have kicked on the first if it was advantageous to his side, but the kick, no doubt, would have been of prodigious length and supremely accurate.

He was the master of his art, so too Ledgard, Bert Cook of Leeds, Hull's Freddy Miller and many more whose kicking was part of their armoury before the modern game. If he was feeling so inclined he could tackle too, but that French problem of 'can I be bothered?' had to be bossed first.

I took Great Britain to play France in Perpignan in 1985 and the guest of honour at the game was Pipette. I was introduced to him by the interpreter and gone were the matador looks and the thick black locks. An elderly gentleman greeted me and as the interpreter told him of the drop-goal at Headingley, when he changed feet, he smiled and gently squeezed my hand as he replied 'I just changed feet' with a shrug of his shoulders, in that very French way.

My lasting and vivid memory of my late hero was as our team was leaving the after-match reception and I waved goodbye to this elderly gentleman who is a legend still in the South of France. This small man - but massive player - waved back and called: "Au revoir Maurice" and with the broadest of smiles shouted "Headinglee" and gave the thumbs up sign as he lit another cigarette. My hero to the end, the magnificent, Puig-Aubert.

	App	Tries	Goals	Pts
France	46	1	150	303

(Puig Aubert may have scored more goals for France, but some records were not available)

Arthur Beetson

Arthur Beetson, or 'Big Artie', the aboriginal giant, first came to our notice in this country when he was suddenly produced, like the proverbial rabbit-out-of-the-hat, against our 1966 touring Lions. He was virtually unknown and his abrasive style and hard, no-nonsense tackling soon had our boys asking 'who is this bloke?' The Australian newspapers hyped him up when they realized his potential and stories of his eating and drinking prowess - 20 hot dogs and a gallon of beer at one sitting - were spread across the national news sheets day after day.

One story had it that Arthur had walked down from the bush and asked for a game, completely out of the blue, and was a knock-out immediately. He was a very big man, six feet three inches and his weight varied from 16 to 20 stones. When down around 16 stones he played in the second-row, when the bulk increased he moved up into the prop position, he was that kind of forward.

In the 1966 series Arthur was on the way up and he made his debut in the Australian side for the third and deciding test in Sydney. He was subbed in that game to allow Dick Thornett to play, but the Australians won the match 19-14, and the Ashes by two games to one. It was in this game that the young Beetson showed how tough he was as he clashed on several occasions with the two hard men on the Great Britain side, Workington's Brian Edgar and St Helens' Cliff Watson. He stood his corner with those two fearsome men and threw down a challenge for the years to come.

But it was under the guidance of the master coach, Jack Gibson, that Arthur blossomed. His style of play had always, from day one, followed the 'English' style, standing up in the tackle and slipping out deft little passes to supporting team mates. His size and powerful running helped but, like all great players, his timing of the pass that did the damage. Who can forget, in the final test of the 1973 tour at Warrington, when, with the game in the balance, and the series at one each, his pass from a three-man tackle that saw the powerful Ken Maddison scorching over to clinch a 15-5 victory and regain the Ashes that Australia had lost in 1970.

Jack Gibson once told me that he rated Arthur as his all-time best Australian prop, as he said, with a smile: "The big guy had every skill in his cupboard, and he was a bit on the tough side". To get that sort of rap from Jack Gibson is an honour indeed.

Arthur also had a spell at Hull Kingston Rovers. It wasn't long, but long enough to introduce himself to one or two handy British forwards who 'tested the water' with big Arthur. One who tells a great story about his clash with Artie is the very well-respected former Bramley prop and accepted hard man, Dave Horn. Dave had an 80-minute run-in with Beetson in a game at Craven Park, Hull. Bramley had taken a good Rovers side all the way and the tussle between Horn and Beetson was even-stevens. The whistle ended the match and the players exchanged handshakes and pleasantries as they vacated the arena. Dave thought: "I'll say well played to Beetson" and walked over, purposefully. He was offering his hand just as Beetson turned to face him. Bang, a right cross put Dave Horn's lights out and the first face he saw on recovering was big Arthur's. "Jeez, Dave mate, I thought you was having a go at me, sorry mate," explained Artie.

I was able to see him close to in the Australia versus Dewsbury game on the 1973 tour because I was assistant coach at Crown Flatt at the time, and his play was magical. His ability to pass the ball accurately under pressure from several tacklers was unbelievable, and the way he held the football in one hand, while pulling the nearest tackler into himself with the other, then putting the one-handed pass around the tackler's body, was poetry in motion.

Arthur accumulated 28 international caps for Australia and captained them on occasion, but he loved his native Queensland as much as his country and it is hard to believe that he only gained one State of Origin appearance. This was due, no doubt, to the fact that Arthur's playing days were almost over when inter-state matches were changed to the State of Origin format of today.

His record in coaching Queensland though is totally different, having been in charge many, many times, notably in 1983 when his Queenslanders won 43-22 in Brisbane to record the highest score to date in State of Origin, and in 1989, when New South Wales were beaten, again in Brisbane by the widest margin, 36-6. The coach of New South Wales in that series was Arthur's best mate and mentor, Jack Gibson.

The last time I saw him he was in his prop forward's mode weighing a good 20-odd stone and the hair was silver grey, but whenever I see him I remember that big, black-haired, rock-hard Queenslander, who put the frighteners on a lot of opponents, Arthur 'hero' Beetson.

	App	Tries	Goals	Pts
Redcliffe	56	13	0	39
Balmain	74	6	1	20
Hull KR	12	1	0	3
Eastern Suburbs	131	17	0	51
Parramatta	18	1	0	3
Queensland	3	0	0	0
Australia	28	1	0	3

Dean Bell

Dean Bell's first game as a Leeds player coincided with my first as Leeds coach. It was in the John Player Special Trophy, a second round tie at Headingley, against the joint favourites for the trophy, Hull Kingston Rovers. 'Deano' played that day as if he had been at Leeds all his career, and had the extreme pleasure of scoring a crucial try late in the first half that put Leeds into a lead which they never lost.

I kept the same team throughout the cup run, which ended with us winning the trophy, beating Widnes in the final. Dean was a key figure and staunch leader in both attack and defence for me. As a youngster making his way in the game, he was always willing to listen and take on board what the coach would suggest. This aspect of his game came from the fact that Dean came from a rugby-playing family and, with its Maori background, had plenty of relations also involved in rugby football.

Cameron Bell, Dean's father, was a good footballer who moved into coaching after playing, and indeed coached in this country for quite a few years, first at Carlisle. Then when the Cumbrian club merged with Barrow, he coached at Craven Park and did a good job too.

Dean's first English club was Carlisle when they were in the old First Division, and I saw him for the first time when I went as a spectator to watch a Leeds versus Carlisle league game at Headingley in 1982. The young Kiwi impressed me immensely with his guts, determination, pace and power. He was by far the young Carlisle club's best player.

His stay in Cumbria was a short one and he returned to New Zealand but came back to Great Britain very quickly when he toured with the Maori side that played tests at amateur level against BARLA. The Leeds directors, remembering the young centre who had starred against them earlier, moved in smartly to sign both Dean and the excellent hooker, Trevor Clark, who later had long spells at Featherstone Rovers and Bradford Northern.

Dean had pace, explosive pace, allied to tremendous upper body strength. He would burst through a defence when it appeared that he was stopped and was also a devastating head-on tackler. Gaining 26 caps for New Zealand, Dean's inspirational coach at international level and later at Wigan, was Graham Lowe. He rated the powerful centre so much that in his early test career he played Dean on the wing, but with a roving commission, allowing him to come inside when the Kiwis were in possession and look for mid-field breaks. This worked a treat for the Kiwis as Dean proved a tricky opponent with his decisive thrusts and astute football brain.

His career also extended to Australia because when Dean represented New Zealand on the 1985 tour of the UK he was in fact playing for the then Eastern Suburbs club, today's Sydney City Roosters. Dean had a very successful spell with Easts and was playing to the top of his game when I returned to the Leeds club after my stint as Great Britain coach.

This coincided with the excellent Graham Lowe's appointment as the new Wigan boss, and we heard on the grapevine that Dean was coming out of contract at Eastern Suburbs. The Leeds board went straight in with a contract offer and because we had had a successful partnership in the 1983-84 season we fancied our chances of landing the superb Kiwi. The tie between Dean and Graham Lowe though was too strong and the New Zealand international decided to go with his former boss to Central Park. This proved to be a masterstroke on Dean's part because it introduced the most successful chapter in his career.

With the famous Wigan club Dean won every medal several times over, in a glittering spell with a side that included stars of the calibre of Ellery Hanley, Martin Offiah, Shaun Edwards, Andy Gregory, Joe Lydon, Va'aiga Tuigamala, Andy Farrell, Jason Robinson, Denis Betts and Gary Connolly. What an array of talent.

Dean did go back to Leeds, but it was as a coach at the end of his wonderful playing career. However, his spell as supremo at that demanding club was not a successful one and he moved sideways to take a job which proved to be excellent for him, that of nurturing and producing young talent within the club, as junior development officer and coach. He was so good at it that Wigan took him back in that capacity and now have a junior system second-to-none.

A hero in anyone's book, Dean Bell, as a player, captain, coach and developer of junior players, is another former player of mine, of whom I am extremely proud.

	App	Tries	Goals	Pts
Carlisle	23	11	0	33
Eastern Suburbs	40+2	8	0	32
Leeds	23	5	0	20
Wigan	244+9	96	0	384
Auckland	19	3	0	12
New Zealand	26	11	0	44

Also played for New Zealand Maoris, North Island and Oceania.

Brian Bevan

When he strode, like a rugby colossus, down the touchline in his heyday, one would hear all around the rugby league grounds as spectators queued for admission to a Warrington game: "Is 'Bev' playing?" He was the man you would pay your two bob to watch and be thrilled by his exploits. He was the man that you wanted to get the ball, no matter who you supported, because things happened when Bev had the ball.

He was the man who knocked on the dressing room door at Headingley, immediately after the Second World War still in his merchant seaman's uniform and asked for a trial for the Leeds club. The then manager looked at the slim wingman, told him to get ready for training, and laughed as he saw this 'bag of bones' pulling on a pair of knee bandages, full of holes, to cover the knobbliest knees he had ever seen. He never made it onto the pitch. "If I were you, I'd try your luck over in Lancashire" was the Leeds boss's advice, so he did, and he became a legend, Brian Bevan, the pencil-thin destroyer, the Australian will-o-the-wisp, the 'bag of bones' that was the most dangerous runner of his generation in rugby league.

The greatest accolade that any person can obtain is that everyone claims to know you personally, you are their mate. In the case of Brian Bevan, they have seen every one of your tries, in fact were there at every game that you scored a try.

What about his tries: all 796 of them. This record was achieved between 1945 and 1964, and in 1952-53, Bev came the nearest to breaking the all-time tries in a season record, held by another Australian, Albert Rosenfeld with 80, when he ran in 72. He scored more than 60 tries in a season on three occasions, over 50 on five, over 40 on three and over 30 on two occasions.

He was a phenomenon. People looked at him and thought: "He will get hurt if he plays". He looked elderly, like someone's dad playing in a charity dads versus lads game, until he got the ball, then everyone had to look out. Bev looked as if he was sitting in an armchair when he ran, so relaxed and at ease. His head was usually leaning back with his chin in the air and his arms pumping and, as is the case with world class players, he always appeared to have lots of space around him, as if there was a scenic barrier surrounding him, keeping tacklers away. If he side-stepped, he would seem to cover several yards with the step, always with the time and space to do whatever he wanted.

How can anyone separate almost 800 tries? He scored so many running the length of the field that they became everyday occurrences. One though is well-documented and was such a superb try that even the hard-to-please Wiganers accepted it as possibly the best they had ever seen. It was such a wonderful try that a sketch appeared in a Wigan newspaper showing the route Bev took to score. Taking possession of the ball inside his own in goal area, by the side of the corner flag, Bev set off on a run that took him over the try line in the diagonal corner, some 110 yards as he ran and the writer in the newspaper marked each spot where he beat a defender, and named the tackler who missed him. People who saw the event reckon that Bev avoided 14 tackles; they say he beat Ces Mountford twice.

I played against Brian Bevan three times and as I recall he scored six tries in those three games, a couple from almost his own try line.

I often wonder just how much he missed playing for Australia in test football. The fact that he could score tries against anyone in the world must surely have qualified him to wear the green and gold jumper. But even for someone of Bev's ability, the Australians stuck to their rule of not selecting players who did not play their club rugby in Australia.

The nearest he ever got to test football was regular selection for that grand team, the Other Nationalities, which boasted the likes of Bev, Lionel Cooper, Arthur Clues, Harry Bath, Dave Valentine, Pat Devery, Trevor Allan and a host of ex-pat Australians, Kiwis, Scots, Irish and any non-British player deemed good enough.

A footnote to any story about Brian Bevan is that after he retired, he lived on the south coast, near Torquay, and a snippet of news appeared in a Torquay weekly paper giving the scorers for the various teams at the Torquay Rugby Union Club. The first, second and third teams were listed as was the Veterans XV, with the leading try scorer, with an outstanding 40-odd tries, one B. Bevan. His deeds on a rugby league field are legend, so is the man, Bev.

	App	Tries	Goals	Pts
Eastern Suburbs	8	0	1	2
Warrington	620	740	34	2,288
Blackpool Borough	42	17	0	51
Other Nationalities	16	26	0	78

Mick Blacker

Here I leave the level of international footballers and household names to mention a player who, like David Cholmondely who appears later in this book, may not be as well known nation-wide as some of the rest, but, as in Cholmondley's case, he would be the man you wanted with you if the going was tough.

A Huddersfield lad, Mick was signed at Odsal when playing for Birkby Youth Club and served a short apprenticeship in the reserves before breaking into the Northern first team. The season of 1972-73 was a big one for him because in October 1972, he was selected for, and played in, the Yorkshire County side that beat Lancashire 32-18 at Castleford. Later that season the Challenge Cup saw Bradford Northern fight their way to Wembley and Mick was at stand-off, as he had been for Yorkshire earlier, when the proud Northern side walked out on that superb Wembley turf. Mick received a runners-up medal as Bradford went down to a good Featherstone Rovers team coached by Peter Fox.

In June 1977, I went as assistant coach with Peter Fox to Odsal. I worked with the excellent 'A' team, and I found a great set of young players, all aching to get in the Bradford first team, with just the right amount of 'old heads' to make the side one of the best in the Yorkshire Senior Competition. Mick Blacker was in and out of the first team, but always gave 100 per cent when he came down to my team.

I got the chance to go to the Halifax club which had run into hard times and needed a kick-start to put them back among the big boys at the top in the First Division. I knew that Peter Fox was interested in the Halifax centre and captain, Lee Greenwood. Lee wanted away from Thrum Hall because it looked as though the club would be ejected from the league unless a miracle saved them, things were so bad financially.

Ron Dobson, the football director, and I negotiated a deal with Northern that brought Mick Blacker to Thrum Hall and Lee Greenwood went to Odsal, a deal made sweeter because Halifax received £1,000 as well. Additionally, we struck up a good relationship with the Bradford chairman, the late Harry Womersley, and he helped us tremendously with cut-price players who, in turn, pulled trees up for Halifax.

I made Mick the captain from day one and he led the team with drive, common sense and enthusiasm. A stocky, strong and powerful runner, Mick also had strength in the tackle and his build allowed him to get beneath the ball carriers' line of balance and his strength gave him the lift to turn the player in mid-air, and perform the perfect crash tackle.

The combination of Ken Loxton, Terry Langton and Blacker working at numbers 13, 7 and 6 respectively gave us the edge on most teams and with us recovering at a great rate, but still in the Second Division, we caught many sides from the First Division cold when meeting us in cup ties, particularly at Thrum Hall.

I can't speak highly enough of the input Mick made to the tremendous seasons we had at Halifax at that time. In our terrific Challenge Cup run of 1979-80, when we reached the semi-final against Hull Kingston Rovers at Headingley while still in the Second Division, Mick was rushed into hospital for an emergency appendix operation after our win at Barrow in the second round. Johnny Blair stood in for Mick in our legendary third round win over Wakefield Trinity, and scored four drop-goals in our 7-3 triumph at Thrum Hall.

I knew that Mick's presence would be sorely missed should he be ruled out of the semi-final. Mick declared himself fit on the Thursday before the big game and we kept it a secret, even from the local newspaper. What a boost it gave, not only to our team, who knew on the Thursday, but to the thousands of Halifax supporters who raised the roof when the teams were announced just before kick-off. It surprised Hull Kingston Rovers too, but they ran out winners 20-7 and our Wembley was the semi-final, with promotion that season as an extra bonus to the wonderful Halifax supporters.

As a coach, I was lucky to have had some superb captains working with me, but none better than Mick Blacker. He left a secure position at Bradford with me only having to ask him to come with me once. There were no questions, he just said "Yes, I'll join you", and that was to go to a club that if we had failed, would have folded. His team responded magnificently to his on-field leadership as the good times returned to the famous Thrum Hall. Mick's captaincy was far in advance of his singing ability as those who were in the Rook pub after we had beaten Barrow in the cup can testify. Mick and Terry Langton volunteered to be back-up singers to Con Clusky of The Bachelors, who gave our team a full spectrum of his hits, with the Halifax half-backs in full voice.

Mick took over as coach with Ken Loxton at Halifax when I left, then went to Warrington with Ken Kelly and finally coached Mansfield Marksmen. Great captain, great hero.

	App	Tries	Goals	Pts
Bradford Northern	196+34	46	0	138
Halifax	130+11	33	2	102
Warrington	38+4	11	0	37
Mansfield	11+3	0	0	0
Yorkshire	1	0	0	0

Dean Blankley

This fine utility player was spotted playing for his home-town junior side, Normanton. This is another of those closely knit former mining centres that are clustered around the Wakefield and Castleford district and while smaller in size than those two, is bigger than its nearby mining neighbours, Sharlston, Streethouse and Snydale. Like the Back o' t' wall ground at Sharlston, Normanton had its own 'house of pain', called Mopsey Garth and this is where the young Blankley learned his trade.

Signed by Castleford in November 1987 as a promising scrum-half, Dean soon made his mark and, despite a couple of injuries, was considered good enough to figure in the first team occasionally. But the regular Castleford half-back was the excellent Bob Beardmore, who was also the team's ace goalkicker, and he took some moving from the spot.

So when that good footballing prop Barry Johnson left Castleford to take over coaching Bramley, he took with him a former teammate and wingman, John Kear as assistant coach. John had looked after the Castleford 'A' team and knew of the promise of Dean Blankley. Dean was transferred to Bramley on 2 November 1990 and joined Kear, who later went on to bigger and better things in coaching, as are well documented elsewhere.

I must admit that when I first saw Dean, he was a little overweight. His disappointments at Castleford had also affected the lad and his transfer to McLaren Field was a lifeline thrown to him at the right time. I was offered the Bramley job as John Kear was leaving to take up a position at the game's headquarters as director of coaching. I went along one Tuesday evening to have a look at the squad I would be working with. John gave me his qualified opinion on the team he was leaving and when he came to Dean, we had a difference of opinion. "He's a good 'un" said John, a future Great Britain coach to me, a former Great Britain coach. "Well John' I've seen him and to be honest I don't rate him," I truthfully declared. I had taken the Dewsbury side to Bramley the season before and Dean had played scrum-half in what could have been his first game for them after his transfer and, to be honest had been almost invisible.

But getting fitter every week, and, I think, taking a bit of time to put him on the right road again, Dean began to play as he used to, and his ability to play in three different crucial positions helped me immensely. At scrum-half, hooker or loose-forward, Dean excelled, and eventually I never considered going into a game without him. Steve Carroll figured as the regular scrum-half and he was a good 'un too but, if he was injured, then Dean slotted in. It was the same at loose-forward, Paddy Lyons, another good player, operated at number 13 for me. But should Paddy be missing, then Dean fitted in there. Hooker is where he played mostly and his dummy-half play was of the highest quality. Strong running, with a low centre of gravity, Dean was very hard to pull down and his astute football brain quickly sparked to any new set piece from the play-the-ball.

One particular set move near the opponents' try line brought many tries for our tough prop, Andy Marson, who would shift any player who encroached into his area when running off Dean's set play, by snarling 'My *** ball', and everyone cleared out of his way. My original opinion, as outlined to John Kear, was soon dispelled once I had worked with Dean. His two tries and all-around great display against First Division Bradford Northern, in a Yorkshire Cup tie at Odsal in 1992 is one game I remember. Another was his outstanding game against another First Division side, Featherstone Rovers, in an 18-all draw in the Regal Trophy at Bramley in 1991.

He was a wonderful player and one who took other players forward with him, which is always the mark of a good 'un. Dean played at Bramley until they disbanded and then had outstanding success after moving back into amateur rugby with first Dudley Hill in the Premier Conference League then nearer home where he transformed a Sharlston team into a superb winning outfit.

I know that he was particularly proud of these successes at Back o' t' wall and on his retirement still supported their endeavours from the touchline. He was not an international, but one of the most honest players I ever had the honour to coach. A very good player too, naturally talented, brave and skilful, he was, as John Kear had advised me, a coach's dream to handle.

His wife Lisa has helped him immensely. When their first child was born, a little girl, she was named Sydney, because she was conceived on holiday in that city. The baby's name caused Bramley's prop, Garry Hall, to utter the famous line: "I've got to get home to put our 'Glasshoughton' to bed". Dean Blankley, footballer, builder, super dad and hero.

	App	Tries	Goals	Pts
Castleford	4+1	0	0	0
Bramley	191+11	53	6	218
Lancashire Lynx	3	0	0	0

Also played for Dudley Hill and Sharlston

Billy Boston MBE

Billy signed for Wigan in October 1953. His childhood background and his hardness in life can be summed up in two words, the area in which he was born, Tiger Bay. According to Phil Melling, rugby league expert and historian, Tiger Bay was possibly named by Portuguese seamen who, when sailing into the very rough waters of the Severn Estuary, likened it to sailing into 'Una Bahia de los Tigres', a Bay of Tigers. World renown as a rough area, being born there and growing up there gives one a head start in the crucial skill of survival, so necessary in the iron hard game of rugby league football.

My personal memories of Billy Boston were in his early years at Central Park of watching him from the terraces. My formative years in the professional game were spent studying and learning its many lessons in the 'A' team at Hull FC, having signed professional in 1953 at the tender age of 17 years, just as Billy had for Wigan.

Whenever possible I would make my way to watch Billy and the Wigan side of that era because they were the entertainers of that decade and produced some wonderful football. It was a sight to see the cherry and white jerseys emerge from the dressing rooms, always looking crisp and spotlessly clean and making the team look twice as big as they really were - and they were already a big set.

Billy took the XIII-a-side code by the scruff of the neck and was an instant success. Big for a wingman then, his pace and power were awesome and his footwork for such a big man was unbelievable. My mind's eye can see him now, hugging the touchline challenging the unlucky tackler to knock him into touch. "Come on, all you have to do is push me into touch" he seemed to say and if the tackler took the bait you could guarantee it would be he who bit the dust.

A powerful hand-off, swerve, change of direction and change of pace, Billy had it all. A glance at the try scoring charts tells us that Billy only topped the list twice, in 1956-57 with 60 tries and in 1961-62 with 51, but the quality of top class wingmen was very high in that period with at least 10 excellent world-class finishers playing at the same time. Another tribute to Billy's ability was the number of wingmen who made a name for themselves by simply doing reasonably well when playing against him.

Leeds had two men who dine out regularly on the stories of the games they played against Billy. Eddie Ratcliffe was a tough, strong lad who was a durable defender and in one game he did the impossible by stopping Billy scoring in a big cup tie. People to this day talk about how Eddie Ratcliffe won the game for Leeds by tackling 'Billy B' out of the game. In another match, the selection of Walt Garside brought groans from the Leeds supporters when, just before the kick off, it was announced that he would face the fearsome Welshman. Walt turned the tables that day because it was he who scored a hat-trick of tries in a thrilling Leeds win.

My only meeting with Billy on the field was around 1960 when I played for Dewsbury at Central Park and our coach, Bert Cook, the former Leeds and New Zealand full-back, had a simple ploy to stop Billy scoring. The game plan was easy: just get as many players as possible to confront Billy when he had the ball, especially near our line. I remember breaking from a scrum, 10 yards from our try line and seeing two tacklers, hanging from Billy like Christmas decorations, and him still moving menacingly towards our line. Gritting my teeth, I flung myself around Billy's standing leg at the same time as our loose-forward hit the top of the pile of bodies, but that dreadful feeling of inadequacy came flooding over us as Billy literally carried four of us over the line for a try in the corner.

Always the same when you meet him, Billy Boston has that remarkable gift of being able to walk with commoners and kings and treat them both the same. Like the other famous wingman with double B initials, Brian Bevan, Billy ended his illustrious career at Blackpool Borough, but it is as a superb, exciting young wing threequarter from Tiger Bay that 'Billy B' is remembered. Between 1954 and 1963 he gained 31 test caps, scoring nine tries in nine tests against the Australians and Kiwis and touring Australasia twice, in 1954 and again in 1963. He scared the Australians to death with his powerful running and in one test against the Kiwis in Auckland scored four tries in a 27-7 win. One of my all-time favourite players and heroes, the one and only, Billy Boston, Billy B.

	App	Tries	Goals	Pts
Wigan	486+2	478	7	1,448
Blackpool	11	5	0	15
Great Britain	31	24	0	72

Chris Brereton

A superb ball-handling prop of the old school - tall and strongly built, Chris fitted wonderfully into the Leeds pack on his transfer from Halifax in 1946. He had joined the Thrum Hall outfit from Liverpool Stanley in 1939 and as Halifax continued in the wartime league, Chris was able to play whenever he could for his own club and not have to turn out for another club as a 'guest' player, as many others did.

But it was as a Leeds prop forward that I remember Chris Brereton - originally a St Helens lad - and his magical handling skills that not only mesmerised the opposition, but also the spectators who loved watching such spectacular tricks. The Leeds front row at that time was Dai Prosser, Con Murphy and Chris Brereton.

To tell Chris's full story would take forever. He was an outstanding character in a game full of them. He looked like a rugby league prop: tough, big and strong.

He looked even bigger to me when, as a youngster playing for my school team, Sacred Heart Roman Catholic on Burley Road, Leeds, Chris came along to give us a talk. It was our first season playing the game and because we were doing well our headmaster, Mr Joe Goodwin, arranged for Chris to come down to school. After a good, long talk and answering questions from our team, he asked Mr Goodwin who was the youngest player in the side which was me. Going out to the front of the class to be introduced to Chris was indeed an honour, but the sheer size of him, when I stood near him, was overpowering. He was huge. My Dad was a big man, but Chris appeared to be twice my Dad's size. He wished me well and shook my hand; I didn't wash my hands for a week afterwards.

His nearest shot at international football was a test trial in 1946. Test trials were matches, usually played midweek, on professional grounds, and two evenly selected teams played in a full-bloodied game for the right to be selected for Great Britain, either in an international match at home, or for a Lions tour place.

Chris was a master ball-handler, a clever distributor who would send the opposition running in all directions as he sold dummy after dummy time after time. In one game against Keighley at Headingley, he caught the ball from the first kick-off, standing on the touchline about 60 yards from the Keighley try line. Holding the ball in one huge hand, Chris stood sideways on to the visiting chasing forwards and, leaning back, took the position of the old discus thrower, apparently about to throw a huge cross-field, one-handed pass. Every Keighley player veered infield to cover the long pass that Chris was about to hurl, but he simply dummied the pass and set off up the touchline only to be overhauled inches short by several Keighley tacklers after giving Chris about 20 yards start over the 60 he had to run. I remember it as though it was yesterday.

I remember another great piece of play that won Leeds a game when Chris made a try out of nothing for Gareth Price, the Leeds centre. He sold four outrageous dummies to trundle 30 yards before giving Price a walk-in try. He made one small boy, who had recently shaken hands with him, very happy.

The move that brought many tries to the Leeds side in those days was one in which Chris would take a tackle deliberately and, on falling, would manipulate the ball to show two dummies, one to Alf Watson and another to Arthur Clues, before hanging out a peach of a hanging pass for the express run of Ike Owens to charge onto the ball and score. That was the brilliance of Chris Brereton.

He was transferred to Keighley and as a Lancashire lad brought up in the industrial north west, always knew the worth of a good trade union. He attempted to start a players union in professional rugby league and worked hard to make it work. But it was not in the interests of the then boards of directors at the clubs where players were so much 'meat on the hoof' and little else. There was no help for him and players were warned not to join this great hearted scheme and it gradually petered out.

Not only was Chris a great player, he was a great landlord in several Leeds pubs. I have been told by many mates who went in Chris's pubs just to see and speak to him, such was his fame and wonderful personality, that when asked: "How did you sell so many dummies?", he replied with a smile: "Years of practice lad, years of practice". My one last wish is that the great Chris Brereton is selling dummies still and may turn to say: "I once shook hands with Maurice Bamford". That would be heroic.

	App	Tries	Goals	Pts
Liverpool Stanley	27	2	0	6
Halifax	112	15	2	49
Leeds	56	8	0	24
Keighley	77	12	0	36

Dave Busfield

A lad from the Heavy Woollen District around Dewsbury and Batley, Dave strangely did not play at the local and famous Shaw Cross club, so well known for producing top professional players, but was signed by Featherstone Rovers from the Earlsheaton Youth Club in Dewsbury. This team was coached by local former Dewsbury and Batley forward, Jack Briggs and David always had a good word for the work Jack did with the youngsters.

Another beautifully built player, David had the physique, pace and skill to have gained international honours and this was shown in the way he forced himself into the Featherstone Rovers team in the Wembley Challenge Cup final of 1974, when the Rovers were beaten by Warrington 24-9. Although only 19-years-old, David had shown the ability to play either in the pack or the backs and was being talked about in the corridors of power at Rugby League headquarters as a possible international when, unfortunately, he sustained a serious leg injury while playing against Dewsbury early in 1975.

He was out for a long spell and it looked as though his promising career had come to an end, but as he struggled to regain his hard-earned place in the Featherstone first team, people were looking at David with other ideas about his immediate future.

I had just joined the Halifax club at Thrum Hall as coach and at the start of the 1978-79 season was searching around the local professional teams for good players to lift the old club out of the doldrums. My chairman, Mr Hughes and football director, Ronnie Dobson, approached Featherstone about transferring David to us and we agreed a fee. 'Bussy' came to Halifax and fitted in perfectly. His confidence returned, so too his pace, and he was soon scoring those long range tries which made his name at Post Office Road.

Playing in a disciplined pack in which each man knew his job gave David that bit of time to find his feet again after his traumatic leg injury and sad loss of form and confidence.

David came to us for a £5,000 transfer fee. That was a lot of money for a club like Halifax in those days to gamble on a player who had to regain so much. But he did regain everything in spades. His interception try against Featherstone in our Challenge Cup run to the semi-final in 1980 will forever remain with me as he strode down the slope, with arm aloft in answer to the jeers from the Rovers supporters, for a 50-yard touchdown that won us the tie. And at Barrow in the second round he scored another long-distance effort, beating several defenders to register another winner will live in the minds of the travelling Halifax supporters who made that historic trip up north.

Another of Bussy's beauties was scored in 1979 at Bramley's McLaren Field in a 12-5 Yorkshire Cup win on our way to the final. Receiving the ball on his own '25' yard line, David burst through a very tight home defensive line to race clear and round the full back in style to run a full 75 yards to the posts, a wonderful effort. But later that great season, on our way to another victory at Keighley on Good Friday evening, David broke his leg again while scoring a close-in try.

Despite that horrendous injury, the big lad came back and was signed by the shrewd Arthur Bunting at Hull FC. Later, David moved on again and landed back in his home town to finish his playing career guiding Dewsbury, along with former centre star Nigel Stephenson, to promotion into the old First Division. David then took a coaching qualification and when he retired from professional rugby, went on to coach in the amateur game and embark on a career in coaching.

As he did as a player, he learned quickly and shortly after retiring from playing he was back at Dewsbury as first team coach. Without much financial assistance, he left the Crown Flatt club and moved across the valley to Mount Pleasant, Batley, as assistant coach to David Ward. As one of the regional coaches in the RFL's National Coaching Scheme when I was running the programme, David was given the opportunity to coach the RAF services side and did so for almost five years. He took his squad on a three match tour of New Zealand and did what many coaches fail to do: his side won all three games, including a one-point win in the one-off test match against the Royal New Zealand Air Force team in Auckland.

As a player, David was selected to play for Yorkshire in the county championship in 1980, but an injury cost him his well-deserved county cap. A superbly balanced runner who was a match winner in his own right David would appear from nowhere to burst through a tackle and go clear. An unselfish player, he would always feed the supporting team mate if in a better position than himself and his skilful handling, allied to his strong running, made him a very dangerous opponent. But it was the courageous way he came back from bad injuries that mark him as one of my heroes, alongside the help he gave me in my early coaching career.

	App	Tries	Goals	Pts
Featherstone Rovers	57+29	28	0	84
Halifax	60+7	22	1	67
Hull FC	2+2	1	0	3
Dewsbury	35+5	4	0	16
Huddersfield	6	0	0	0
Wakefield Trinity	2+1	1	0	3

John Cave

Stanningley ARLFC. John Cave is on right of the back row.
Maurice Bamford is second from the left, back row.

I have included John Cave in my list of heroes for three main reasons. First, along with Don Ellis, John was the best all-round amateur loose-forward that I ever played with, or against. John and Don Ellis had so much in common. Both were big, strong, brave men, both were great leaders on the field and if John had the edge anywhere it was in his pace.

Secondly John did play in some excellent Stanningley sides, but he was at the club when things were not so good. He never left even when, in some periods, he was the only class player the side had. Thirdly, for many years he was the yardstick for the younger Stanningley players.

As he began to 'fill out' and his weight increased, John moved up into the front row and played a long time at open side prop. He is a big lad. He would put his six feet two inches, 15 stone frame about as a hard, give-it, take-it forward whose philosophy was "You have to see if they will lie down or fight back".

He usually tested the opposition early on to see what they would do. John was a street fighter too. Never one to back down, no matter what or who the opposition, he was built for that job, and while winning the vast majority of his battles, carried the scars of those battles on his face. Although a tough nut, when it came to playing rugby league he, again like Don Ellis, had become more of a pure footballer as he approached the end of his excellent career. His forté was to appear to be running flat out as he took the ball into the defence. But with a sudden acceleration into the gap between two tacklers, he would take the ball behind their line of defence and, if the support came with him, John would offload the perfect pass to put the supporting player clear. He was a master at that skill.

John went to play for the Leeds club's junior side on leaving school and played for the Leeds 'A' team on several occasions. The first time his nose was broken was when playing for Leeds against Wakefield Trinity 'A' and a renowned puncher flattened it with a haymaker.

John worked as a builder for his father, Harry, who ran a business in Bramley for many years and, on realising that playing professional rugby league may take up too much time from the family business, he went to play for his local club in the amateur game, Stanningley. There he became a member of a cracking side that won its way through to meet Featherstone Rovers in the Challenge Cup first round proper in 1964.

The success of the side was based on a tough pack of forwards and an equally tough set of backs. No one messed with Stanningley in those days. Leon Harrison, Harold Oddy, John Bedford, Keith Norman, Bob Skaife, Jacky Shaw, Terry Smith and, of course, John Cave made up a fearsome pack, with the tough Trevor Elliott, Len Thompson, Jeff Bell, Peter Lorriman and Phil Ascough among the backs. John had the knack of scoring vital tries in cup ties and other big matches. His tough attitude was seen when, as player-coach at Stanningley, I took a team that included John, to play Fryston Welfare in Castleford. It was in a Yorkshire Cup tie and we won a hard match by around two or three points.

The following week we went again to Fryston, this time in the league, but John was out injured. He came to cheer us on, but standing on the touchline was a hard case non-playing opposition supporter who was often seen shouting the odds at games, but never chose to play. He must have thought that John looked harder than he actually was because he picked John out to ridicule him. Suddenly, in a wink, it was all over, the supporter was no longer shouting and John simply continued to watch the game and shout for the lads. The hard case was wheeled away for treatment into the Welfare club.

Another side to John the player was when the old Hunslet club, in its latter days at the grand old Parkside ground, was faced with a players strike. Threatened with expulsion from the Rugby Football League if they postponed their fixture with Bramley, Hunslet contacted the good amateur clubs in Leeds to ask their help in putting out a team to play Bramley. John Cave rallied the amateurs, who were a bit sceptical of playing against the rugged Dave Horn and the quicksilver Johnny Wolford of Bramley. John played at prop himself, took on the mighty Horn head-to-head, and covered himself in glory.

Still building and still looking fit enough to play, John Cave is the epitome of many players who graced the amateur game for years. Most teams and the various amateur leagues have their legends, most of them are characters in their own right and without being boastful, I know most of them. All are great kids. But take my word, John Cave was a special player and a very special friend. When I first played against him, although I never thought I would ever say it, he was and still is, one of my heroes.

John Cave played for Stanningley and made one appearance for Hunslet against Bramley on 9 September 1970.

David Cholmondely

"David who?" I hear you ask after reading about such famous names as Billy Boston and Eric Ashton. David Cholmondely, or 'Chum', also known as 'Clark Kent', a name I will explain later. Let me tell you about this quiet, well-spoken young centre who played for my Halifax and Bramley teams. I had just gone to a struggling Thrum Hall side as coach and, with a very small budget, had to be very selective on whom I approached to sign. Usually the fee I offered was laughed at and the player walked away in disgust.

One Sunday morning I was up and about as usual, finding an amateur game to watch in case there was a budding international who had been missed by the big clubs' scouts, when I saw a game in progress on the Bramley Fall Woods pitch at the side of the Leeds and Bradford Road. Watching the game, I noticed a centre, nicely built, good on his feet and a strong tackler. I looked for his ability to beat a man front on and he could do that too, I also noticed that an opposition forward gave him a clout and his response was to take a look at who it was, wait a while, then just when this bully thought he was clear, the centre let him know he hadn't forgotten with a rib-crunching tackle, had a quick word with him and left him on the ground gasping for air.

Lovely, I thought. I had a quiet word with my mate, Billy Slater, who knew all the players in the team, Bramley Social Club - and Billy agreed that this player had something - so I contacted him, and signed the most honest of footballers who ever pulled on a boot. It was David Cholmondely, Chum to his mates. He came to Thrum Hall, brave, keen as mustard and raw as a carrot.

To blood him, I played him on the wing, letting him get used to the extra pace of professional football and letting him see from the wing position just what was required in the centres. After extensive discussions with his wife, Jane, she decided that it was time David went into the centre. It was the finest selection Jane ever made and Chum and his team never looked back. The Clark Kent name came when the team started to notice a change come over Chum as he stripped into his football gear. Before he gradually got down to putting on his jersey, he first took off his rimless spectacles, put them away and pulled on the blue and white hooped shirt of Halifax. Suddenly gone was the nice, wholesome image of this cracking lad. In its place was a battled-hardened, tough professional rugby player, who had changed facially and physically. He was, without doubt, a Jekyll and Hyde character but, because of the spectacles and being in a more modern time the nickname, Clark Kent, was introduced, obviously because of his glasses and his likeness to Superman, both in looks and how he played.

His partnership with Graham Garrod, in the centres at Thrum Hall, was in the traditional classical mould of those days: Garrod the tall balanced copybook runner and tackler and Chum, the powerbreaker and knock-'em-down defender who complimented Garrod perfectly. There were no frills with Chum, when hit hard, there was never a moan, but rest-assured, retribution was always taken.

He was quite an accomplished goalkicker too, but in one particular game at Rochdale Hornets, the home side had removed our main goal kicker, Jimmy Birts, from the equation. He was in the land of nod, with concussion from a rather high tackle. We won a penalty kick, in front of the Rochdale posts and I was on the field at the time acting as physio. Our players were milling around like lost sheep; who will take this vital kick at goal? There were only minutes left in the game and the score was 7-7, kick this simple goal and we had won. "Chum", I called, "You take it". He lined the kick up, as he had done hundreds of times for Bramley Social, ran up, stroked the ball sweetly, and missed. The game ended at 7-7, the club got a point and the lads got winning money for a draw away from home.

Three years later I signed Chum for Bramley, on a short-term deal that was part of a piece of professional sleight of hand. He came to me from Halifax, then after a few games I transferred him to another club, who I knew wanted Chum and my club Bramley made money on the deal, as did Chum, plus I got a second-rower I wanted in the deal, so all was well.

I had explained to Chum the ins-and-outs of the deal before he came to me and he agreed. Jane, my co-selector, went on to be a head teacher at a school and Chum did well in business. Never an international, but he was a hero to me.

	App	Tries	Goals	Pts
Halifax	136+2	22	24	114
Bramley	19	1	0	3
Keighley	47+2	3	58	123
Southend Invicta	30	4	28	65
Sheffield Eagles	43+6	5	16	47

Clive Churchill

Of all the great players produced in Australia, Clive Churchill is the epitome of all things good in their game. A physically small man, but very strong, 'The Little Master' was the first choice on the Kangaroos' team sheet for many years, not only because of his position, that of full-back on top of the list, but because of his all-round football knowledge and his scrupulously clear attitude on fair play and playing the game within the laws' guidelines. He also had a tigerish will to win and this was passed through to all the players who played with him.

He made his name at the South Sydney inner-city club, renowned for the for the endless belt production of city-born players. It was a club, because of its geographical position, that was always in the eye of the rugby league mad Sydneyites. Souths were well-known, in their club colours of red and green hoops, as they were among the first to join the new Sydney rugby league competition when it formed in 1908. Souths' first ground was known as Nathan's Cow Paddock, but it soon changed to the traditional home of South Sydney, a feared venue, Redfern Oval. Winning the first two titles in 1908 and 1909, gave the club an early impetus and laid the foundation for a tremendous future.

The players who wore the coveted red and green jumpers reads like a "Who's Who" of Australian rugby league: Harold Horder, Cec Blinkhorn, George Treeweeke, Jack Rayner, Len Cowie, Ron Coote, Ian Moir, Bob McCarthy and the greatest of them all, Clive Churchill. Churchill's inbred football skills, his crowd-pleasing style of play and his small stature that enhanced a boyish aura, led to his nickname of The Little Master. When he made his South Sydney debut in 1947, the club was on the brink of a golden era as, with Churchill at full-back, South Sydney lifted the title no fewer than five times from 1950 to 1955, missing out in 1952.

But it was as a youngster of 12 years old that I saw Churchill play in green and gold at Headingley against Leeds in 1948 and I still recall his deeds with clarity. His timing of the tackle when confronted by much bigger opponents was immaculate, as was his running off the centres from an attacking scrum. His vision and reading of the situation and arriving at the correct decision made him a giant despite his diminutive physique. His runs from full-back were like a scalpel cut, slicing open the opponents' defences, his balance while running and the side-step he used to put himself in the clear were trademarks of this wonderful entertainer.

I also witnessed the first test of the 1948 series when Great Britain held out to win 23-21 at Headingley, which was Churchill's first test for Australia against Great Britain. Churchill made the second of his three tours in 1952 and was again the top performer even though the side lost the test series by two games to one. The 1956 tour was the last as a player for Churchill and indeed he retired from test football following the first test defeat at Wigan 21-10, his 13th international against Great Britain.

Back he came though in 1959 as the Australian tour coach with a side that was arguably the best of its kind ever to leave Australia containing players of the calibre of Ken Barnes, Reg Gasnier, Brian Carlson, Brian Hambly, Noel Kelly, Elton Rasmussen, Harry Wells, Ian Walsh, Dud Beattie and Johnny Raper. The Australians gave our boys a lesson in the first test and stormed to a 22-14 win at Swinton's Station Road.

The British selectors went to town for the second test at Headingley and out went forwards Dick Huddart, Mick Martyn and Derek Turner, along with backs Eric Fraser, Billy Boston, and Alex Murphy. What strength Great Britain had in those days: in came backs Ike Southward and Jeff Stevenson. The pack was Abe Terry, Tommy Harris, Don Robinson, Brian McTigue, Don Vines and John Whiteley. Great Britain won a tough encounter 11-10 and in one fracas, Aussie hooker Ian Walsh was knocked out of the scrum by Brian McTigue and coach Clive Churchill, forever anti-British where test football was concerned, considered the action as "the most despicable act ever seen on a test match field".

Clive Churchill lost his final battle with cancer in August 1985 and his funeral at the Cathedral in Sydney was testament to his popularity when the city's roads were closed because of the crowd paying final tribute to The Little Master.

	App	Tries	Goals	Pts
South Sydney	164	13	75	193
New South Wales	27	4	18	48
Australia	34	0	10	20

Terry Clawson

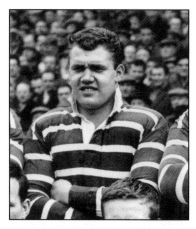

Of all the footballing forwards produced by Featherstone Rovers, Terry Clawson ranks with the best. That he made the grade after a debilitating serious illness took him out of the game for a period, is testimony itself to his courage, fortitude and determination. Signing as a youngster, 'TC' made the first team at Post Office Road in 1957-58 as a line-busting runner playing in the second-row. A big, robust forward, Terry's ability to pick up short passes and straighten onto a ball made him difficult to stop, particularly near the try line and, being a local lad, he soon became a favourite with the Featherstone supporters. He played in a Featherstone pack that included the late Willis Fawley at hooker, and Terry rated Willis as the hardest man he played with or against.

While still a young man he became ill with a chest and lung complaint and was sent to convalesce in Switzerland. Luckily for all concerned he recovered completely, but the illness cost him over a year out of football.

The first two of his 14 Great Britain caps were awarded against France in 1962 as a Featherstone player. The gap between those caps and his next must be close to being a record, because his third was won 10 years later when, in 1972, as a Leeds player he was a key man in the World Cup-winning team in the competition played in France. In that famous success, Terry played in three of the four games required to win the World Cup and was the anchorman of the scrum at open-side prop. Being a superb goalkicker and having kicked over 100 goals in a season several times at various clubs, Terry kicked six goals in the 27-21 win against Australia in the first round win in Perpignan, two crucial goals against France in the 13-4 win in Grenoble and two superb goals in the vital decider against Australia in the 10-all draw in Lyon.

One outstanding feature of his career was the number of accolades he received from both team mates and opposing players when asked: "Who do you rate as the best prop?" Well, in Terry's time there were some tremendous prop forwards around, but the name Terry Clawson always cropped up as one of the best.

He was back on international duty again in 1973 when, as an Oldham player, he played in all three tests against the touring Australians, then in two tests against the French in early 1974. He achieved most things in the game, with Wembley appearances, county games for Yorkshire, and the pinnacle of selections, a Lions tourist in 1974.

Terry clashed with the best in the international field, the fearsome Australian duo of John O'Neill and Bob O'Reilly, the world rated Arthur

Beetson and the three tough Kiwis, Lindsay Proctor, Wayne Robertson and Doug Gailey. He played in four of the six tests on the 1974 tour and in 13 of the 28 games, kicking 24 goals. But his reputation in this country and the respect in which he is held is surely the best measure of his terrific career, which ended at international level after the 1974 tour.

His club career continued at Featherstone after his illness and then he moved to Bradford Northern, followed by Hull Kingston Rovers. His time there saw Terry unable to get among the trophies but he kicked 114 goals for the club in the 1970-71 season. The following season saw a transfer to Leeds and again he managed 120 goals in that 1971-72 season. In May 1972 Leeds went through to play St Helens at Wembley, but it was a runners-up medal for Terry as the Yorkshire side were beaten 16-13. However, he had a winner's medal from the World Cup win in France.

It was onto the Watersheddings at Oldham next as the Lancashire outfit bolstered up their pack by signing the big prop and it was from there that Terry won nine of his treasured Great Britain caps plus selection for the 1974 tour.

A magnificent forward, I played against him several times when he was making his way as a young Featherstone lad and can vouch for his power on the run. He would have done more, if that were possible, but for the illness that stymied his progress, but his presence in the Featherstone pack alongside big Mal Dixon, and running off the ball distribution of the outstanding Don Fox made it obvious that Terry Clawson was a star in the making.

Terry is a role model to what can be achieved by determination and willpower. To meet head on the problems that threatened his early career and the way in which he overcame them is a pointer to us all. He became a leading world class forward, respected and revered and could dish it out and take it without moaning.

He climbed the mountain and came down the other side and in doing so became a legend in his time in rugby league football. The Australians rated him highly and always speak of him in glowing terms. Nobody messed with TC, the Great Britain forward from a pit village who became a hero to all in the game.

	App	Tries	Goals	Pts
Featherstone Rovers	215	41	483	1,089
Bradford Northern	147+6	16	246	540
Hull KR	110+1	9	204	435
Leeds	62	5	159	333
Oldham	22	1	26	55
York	28	2	4	14
Wakefield Trinity	8+1	0	2	4
Huddersfield	3	1	0	3
Hull	2	0	0	0
Yorkshire	9+1	0	3	6
Great Britain	14	0	25	50

Arthur Clues

One of my personal heroes - as a boy I wanted to be Arthur Clues. Not a film star, or a millionaire, but Arthur Clues. I idolised the man. I remember reading in the *Yorkshire Evening News*, that this young Australian international forward had arrived in Leeds and would be playing against Hull at Headingley on the following Saturday. A group of excited youngsters, me included, set off that winter's evening to walk up Cardigan Road to the Mecca of rugby league with the prime object of looking at this giant Aussie who had supposedly fought and beaten every Great Britain forward on the recent tour of Australia in 1946, as he trained with his new team for the first time.

The terrible winter of 1946-47 had not yet arrived, but snow was in the air as we arrived to find hundreds of spectators already there. I remember one chap, a Bramley supporter, who said: "I wish we could get this many to watch our team, never mind one player." That was the undying charisma of big Arthur.

Photographs in the evening papers weeks later showed him eating the snow, which by then was several feet deep, because he had never seen it before. He played his first game against a tough Hull outfit and although in a team beaten by a few points, he was obviously a star. He was well over six feet tall and well proportioned - tough with a touch of pace one would expect from an international player. He had an exceptionally good kicking game and his two specialities were the long kick to touch, usually from an impossible angle and the short chip over, which he collected on the first bounce and away he went. The latter was a killer, as teams would come up in one defensive line and Arthur would run at them, kick over and be away before they realised the danger. From this break the support players would stream through and Arthur, always the good footballer, would lay on the scoring pass.

In the three test matches in Australia in 1946, Arthur had tangled with most of the British pack, and backs too if they challenged him, notably the Bradford Northern centre, Jack Kitching. However, it was his tussles with the Wigan hooker, Joe Egan, Doug Phillips the Oldham second-rower and Frank Whitcombe the Bradford Northern prop that hit the headlines over here.

Because of his reputation and his ability as a player, Arthur was a target for lesser men who attempted to rile him into getting sent off, but in those days the referees took a different line. The game had a certain more old-fashioned 'give a knock, take a knock' style than today. For instance many a time a referee would see a slap or punch and would say to the receiving player: 'Leave it now, Johnny, it's one apiece. I saw you give him one earlier'. Nine times out of 10 that would be the end of it.

But a lot had hung over from that 1946 tour, Arthur was alone over here in England and he had to be forever on his guard as the British tourists took retribution for the happenings on tour.

Arthur had a little side step that he used occasionally; it was more a change of direction, a little prop off either leg to the left or right, a beauty of a step. I was 10 years old when Arthur arrived and he was 21. Yet as a 21-year-old myself, I played against Arthur twice when he had gone to Hunslet, and on the first occasion I found myself wondering how on earth I had managed to be on the same field as him, my childhood hero. I soon found out I was on the field after he gave me a backhander across the chops though, because I had been lucky enough to make two early breaks, and the touch-up he gave me was just to let me know he was there. "We don't want any more of them young 'un," he growled, and through respect, I concurred.

The second time I was more at ease and he actually sought me out at the end to shake hands and have a kindly word: "Keep trying for those breaks young 'un," he advised, "but don't forget to keep your head down afterwards". He had remembered me. Big Arthur knew I existed. It made my year.

When I coached at Leeds during my second spell there, Arthur would come along to my office, have a coffee, and also have me in stitches with tales about the old days both here and in Australia. He never lost his Australian twang and I always kidded him that he was the only professional Australian in the world. A wide user of superlatives in his conversations, no matter who the company, he was accepted as being Arthur Clues, Australian, and I never knew of anyone taking umbrage over his ultra-colourful language.

He was brilliant, a bright star that lit up our game in the austere days just after the Second World War, and a character who was fun to be with. He was a legend who came from Australia for a short spell and stayed for life, a magnificent forward and, as he would have put it, 'one hard bastard'.

He was my hero when I had two heroes, Arthur and my Dad. Arthur died a few years ago, but I can see him still, a real hero!

	App	Tries	Goals	Pts
Western Suburbs	50	17	2	55
Leeds	236	74	0	222
Hunslet	83	12	0	36
New South Wales	5	0	0	0
Australia	3	0	0	0
Other Nationalities	14	2	0	6

Lionel Cooper

Of the many wingmen who impressed me as a youngster watching the game in the post-war 1940s, such as Bradford Northern's Eric Batten, Leeds's Walt Best, Wigan's Johnny Lawrenson and Warrington's Brian Bevan, the one who became an instant hit with me was Lionel Cooper. His very name conjures up the image of the typical Australian, because he was big, fair haired, handsome, with that cheery, cheeky way they spoke and a breezy attitude to life in general.

Lionel first came to my notice when reports of the Lions test matches were radioed in from Australia in 1946. The Lions had been beaten by the ultra-tough Newcastle District side the week before the first test at the Sydney Cricket Ground. It was normal to rough up the tourists with this hard fixture against the coal miners of Newcastle, just before the first test. It almost worked, as the Lions were pushed all the way to secure an 8-8 draw in the test match. Cooper scored the best of the four tries registered, with a typical blockbusting run, scattering several would-be tacklers and bringing the 65,000 crowd to its feet. Aussie centre Bailey scored their other try. Frank Whitcombe and the magnificent Willie Horne replied for the Lions. Gus Risman and Joe Jorgenson landed a goal each.

Cooper went on to score the Australians' try in the second test in Brisbane in a 14-5 win for the Lions, and indeed, played in the third test in Sydney where a 20-7 win gave the Lions the Ashes.

In early 1947 a ban on the movement of players between Australia and Great Britain was introduced, but Cooper just beat it when he signed for the superb Huddersfield club and arrived to grace the magnificent Fartown ground until his retirement from the game as a player in 1955. When one remembers the great Huddersfield side of that era, a three name combination immediately springs to mind: Cooper, Hunter and Devery. What magic memories there are of those three wonderful players. Johnny Hunter was an inspirational full-back and Pat Devery a wonderful footballing utility middle back who had played at number six in all three tests in 1946 with Cooper. Hunter was considered as a travelling companion for Cooper and, dare I say, was regarded as a makeweight in the deal that brought Cooper over. The pair cost the Fartowners a princely £1,500. This was without doubt the best bit of business done in the game's history.

The excitement generated by these two players and Devery, filled Fartown regularly and when I was coach at Fartown in 1980 I spoke to a former international player who still came to support his old club. Looking out at the old long terrace he told me: "In the 1948 season we played

Warrington on the Saturday, the Australian tourists on the following Wednesday and Wigan at home the next Saturday. Three top games and the lowest crowd that week was 22,000." This shows the quality of play served up by this Huddersfield side, with Lionel Cooper as the main drawing card. In his time at Huddersfield, Cooper scored 432 tries and, in one game against Keighley in November 1951 registered 10 tries and two goals for 34 points.

To see the big wingman, six feet two inches and 15 stones, careering, like a runaway train down the touchline, travelling at a fair rate of knots, with a rocking motion as he ran, was an awesome sight. His hand-off was likened to a steam-hammer and another couple of lethal weapons were his hips. Allowing a tackler to come into him with an attempted leg tackle, he would sway into his opponent, hit him with a big nudge, quickly regain his good balance and be on his way to the try line.

When I was playing as a junior at Headingley, the club would conduct regular 'meet the stars' sessions for us and bring along various top players to talk and offer us a question and answer session. Lionel came once and mesmerised us with his know-how and tales of derring-do. I never had the honour of playing against him, but do feel proud that Lionel Cooper was the coach at Dewsbury who signed me from Hull FC in 1957.

All three of the super Australians at Huddersfield were tremendously popular and they all returned home to Australia soon after retiring from the game. Lionel Cooper had a strong connection with the colour gold. He wore the green and gold of his country and the claret and gold of his chosen English club. I think he did because he was a golden player and one who must rank as one of the all-time greats in an era of all-time greats: Lionel Cooper, Huddersfield and Australia.

	App	Tries	Goals	Pts
Eastern Suburbs	27	14	0	42
Huddersfield	336	420	42	1,344
New South Wales	4	6	0	18
Australia	3	2	0	6
Other Nationalities	14	13	0	39

Keiron Cunningham

Coming from a family of very good rugby league players, it was always on the cards that Keiron would make the grade. Eddie, one older brother, played for Lancashire, Wales and Great Britain in representative football and St Helens, Wigan, Widnes and Batley in club rugby. Another brother, Tommy, played for St Helens, Warrington and Wales. Eddie played mostly in the centre but could also get by at loose forward, while Tommy was, like Keiron, a hooker.

The St Helens area has produced a host of great rugby league players from each era of the game and indeed even provided Mr J. H. Houghton as joint manager of the first two Lions Tours in 1910 and 1914.

Keiron is the modern-day, king-pin number nine: strong in defence, with a superb eye for an opening on attack. His strength, when running near the opposition line, is awesome and his midfield breaks put the opposition defence on the back foot, thus creating chances for the Saints to perform their wonderful support play and excite their thousands of admirers. Most of Keiron's runs come from the dummy half position and he is arguably the most dangerous attacker from that position in the game today.

Can we compare Keiron to any of the great hookers from the past? Well any comparisons are hard to make because the game, particularly as a hooker, has changed so much in the years since competitive scrums were the norm. Is Keiron as good as say, Wigan's Joe Egan? Well, taking into account that time lends enchantment, Joe did not have the match-winning, explosive power possessed by Keiron and, in a different era, Keiron does not have Joe's footballing guile, or the ability to drive his team around the field from dummy half, but with the six tackle rule in force, as opposed to unlimited tackles in Joe's day, that last comparison is not an option. Would Keiron have managed in competitive scrums against the physical hardness of say, Tony Fisher or Featherstone's Willis Fawley and Castleford's Clive Dickenson? Make no mistake, scrums in the days of competitive huddles were a very different ballgame than today. Self-preservation for the hooking fraternity was vital in those hard days of heads clashing at every scrum, being pressurised by the opposing open-side prop, who attempted to upset the opposing hooker at each scrum by using his head, fist or knee, or by the hard-case number nine who faced you in the middle.

But don't confuse dirty play with the jobs that props and hookers had to learn. Bill Sayer, who played for Wigan and St Helens, was not only a hard man, versed in the ways of putting off an opposing hooker, he was also a skilled technician in the art of ball-winning. Peter Clarke and Colin Clarke had this skill, as did any hooker of note in those very different times. But today one must ask if the old-style hooker could compare with Keiron and, sadly, I think some would come through the comparison well, but not all. Today's hooker needs to be much more than a ball-winner or dummy-half specialist. Keiron's opposition today comes mainly in the shape of the excellent pair of Wigan's Terry Newton and Leeds's Matt Diskin. All three are much, much more involved in the broken-field play than previous rakes were.

So, as we accept that the modern game has changed the playing characteristics of hookers and props to almost unrecognisable proportions, I would then ask how Keiron and his modern-day band of hookers would have faired against those who were around just before the change of styles, such as David Ward, David Watkinson, Kevin Beardmore and current Great Britain coach Brian Noble? The two fastest running hookers I ever saw were Colin Clarke and Dewsbury's Mick Stephenson, 'Stevo' of television fame. Both were as quick as backs and still did their work in the pack and in the loose. But no matter what talking points we raise, the fact is that, in most experts' opinions, Keiron Cunningham is currently one of the best, if not the best, hookers in the world.

The Australians and New Zealanders always produce top hookers but for sheer enjoyment to watch and a pure adrenalin rush whenever he picks up the ball, Keiron Cunningham must be included, not only as today's top hooker, but as one of our best ever number nines.

Considering the quality hookers we have produced over the years, that is a big statement but his power-play and the way he lifts his St Helens and international team mates is surely a top gift. Keiron is a hero to the fanatical St Helens supporters and is a very heroic player when in the red and white of Saints, red of Wales or red, white and blue of Great Britain.

	App	Tries	Goals	Pts
St Helens	301+5	129	0	516
Lancashire	1+1	0	0	0
Great Britain	11	1	0	4
Wales	7+3	2	0	8
(To end 2004 season)				

Willie Davies

Our game was made the poorer when the fabulous Welsh half-backs and centres ceased leaving the valleys and industrial towns of the principality to take the 'trek' up North. In most cases it was the silver shilling that attracted these exciting runners and wonderful kickers of the ball to leave family and lifelong friends behind and live amongst the tall factory chimneys, the grime and the folk who spoke a strange dialect that included words like 'thee', 'tha' and 'laikin'.

One of the finest players to make the trip was W. T. H. Davies; Willie Davies of the twinkling sidestep, the sharp acceleration into the narrowest of gaps, the dummy that had defenders bewildered, the swerve that was reminiscent of a ghostly encounter and the speed away once into the gap. Then the hands came into play and his were the safest and cleverest pair, like those of a magician, and after creating openings galore, those sweet passes would send his two Bradford Northern centres, the brilliant Ernest Ward and the awesome, big Jack Kitching, striding away.

A master tactician, Willie had the benefit of a superb rugby union background on which to hone his repertoire of skilful kicks and many tries were scored from these as he would place the ball, diagonally across the field or, as we used to say, 'on a tanner' for the likes of Eric Batten and Emlyn Walters to zoom onto, from the wing positions, pick up and usually score with ease.

Born in the small cockle fishing village of Penclawd, on the Gower coast, Willie was the quintessential Welsh fly-half, born to the game, and with that inbuilt skills expertise so much in evidence in Welsh rugby union stars such as Cliff Morgan, Barry John and Phil Bennett. He wrote his name early in Welsh rugby union folklore when, aged just 19, he and his cousin the wonderful Haydn Tanner, who was still at school, played at stand-off and scrum-half, for Swansea against the fearsome New Zealand All Blacks in an 11-3 win for Swansea. Both had excellent games in a victory that stunned the rugby-playing world.

But, in 1939 Willie came north and joined the Odsal-based team that was to become among the best of its day. Willie's long-term half-back partner was the vastly underrated, Donald Ward, brother of Great Britain captain Ernest.

The crowds rolled up to see this superb Northern side and witness the expert craftsman Willie Davies at work. In this era of brilliant stand-off halves - such as Dicky Williams, Ces Mountford, Ray Price, Willie Horne and Ron Rylance - Willie Davies was one of the best. He was never better than the day he won the coveted Lance Todd Trophy as the best and fairest player in the 1947 Challenge Cup Final at Wembley, against my heroes, Leeds. Northern won that encounter 8-4 and I still recall the radio commentator's voice as my Dad and I sat glued to the wireless. "And it's Davies again, cutting the Leeds defence to shreds as he sprints clear and has Walters with him. Davies draws Cook to him and passes to Walters who goes in at the corner flag," he called. I was heartbroken, my team was being cleaned out by Willie Davies. "Where was Dickie Williams to allow Davies to make that try?" I demanded from my Dad. He slowly lit his Woodbine and explained so simply to me that I never forgot the reason: "Davies is a class player lad, he has beaten better players, man-to-man, than Dickie".

Willie also gained many rugby league caps for Wales as they held their own in those days in the very entertaining European Championship. Willie's regular partner in the Welsh side at scrum-half was the clever, experienced Dai Jenkins, and a very strong Welsh team in 1947 included: Tuss Griffiths, Gareth Price, Roy Francis, Frank Whitcombe, Trevor Foster, the captain, Mel Meek, Doug Phillips and the brilliant Ike Owens. What a team.

My final memory of Willie Davies is of standing with my Dad on the cinder hill, behind the posts at the Rooley Lane end of Odsal with snow falling heavily and the light fading fast, as he sliced through a tiring Leeds defence and, running towards us while using Trevor Foster as a foil with the cheekiest of dummies, dived over for superb solo try that beat Leeds on the day.

As a kid going to and from school we used to pass Dai Jenkins's house in Cardigan Road, Leeds and on occasion actually spoke to the great man. I remember distinctly to our question of "Dai, who is the best stand off you have played against?" the answer was, without hesitating: "Willie Davies, he could do everything well!"

That was good enough for me, coming from Jenks. Good enough indeed to make the superb Willie Davies a hero of mine.

	App	Tries	Goals	Pts
Bradford Northern	237	55	2	169
Wales	9	1	0	3
Great Britain	3	0	0	0

Des Drummond

This superbly athletic wingman, whose career embraced 24 Great Britain international caps, played most of his club football at Leigh and had shorter spells at Warrington and Workington Town. He was a truly remarkable athlete, and was known as the 'Bolton Bullet'. A winner of several stages of the high-profile BBC multi-event sports show, *Superstars*, in which the contestants from all the top professional sports competed, Des just failed to emulate another rugby league star, Keith Fielding of Salford, in winning the competition outright.

But it was his skill as a devastating finisher and crunching defender that made his name in the hard-knock game of top professional rugby league. Des was not a big man, far from it, but he was beautifully balanced and very, very strong. Another tremendous asset was his speed off the mark; he could hit the straps very quickly, as he once proved when playing for Leigh against my Leeds team in the Regal Trophy semi-final, at Huddersfield, in December 1983. With the game just about even, Leigh won a set scrum about 40 yards from our tryline and 10 yards from the touchline. Leigh's Kiwi international scrum-half, Shane Varley, shot down the blind side of the scrum, drew our wingman, Andy Smith, and let loose Des with a perfect pass. Down the touchline sped the flying Drummond, then veered inwards towards our full-back, Ian Wilkinson. As Wilkinson hesitated a split-second to weigh up his challenge, Des raced outside again to round the floundering full-back in a flash and swallow dive in at the corner flag for a wonderful try.

Fred Lindop was the referee and he was quick for a non-player, but Des was so fast away that the referee was miles behind him and, as Des hit the air in his dive, Fred was already pointing for a try. Our covering tacklers turned as one in an appeal against the try, signalling that Des had dropped the ball, but Lindop was adamant that the score would stand. Later newspaper photos and the early form of video recordings, show Des losing the ball completely when about three feet in the air and the ball bouncing over the touch-in-goal line for what should have been a 'no try' decision. The wingman's speed and the clinical way he turned Wilkinson inside out, I suppose, was worth a try and, as we won the game anyway, it didn't matter in the long run, but it the typical Drummond magic.

In defence he was awesome. Many an opponent, not knowing him, would target Des to run at because of his size, and what a mistake they had made. They would suddenly find themselves going upwards and backwards at a fair rate of knots, as Des produced one of his crash tackles.

It was this sort of teeth-loosening, mind-befuddling tackle made on the New Zealand captain and world class second-rower, Mark Graham, during the first test that Great Britain lost to the Kiwis at Headingley that won us the second test at Wigan in the 1985 series. Because of that massive crash tackle, Graham was unfit to play and the Kiwis badly missed his leadership. Garry Schofield's four tries helped us a bit too.

Des was a member of the Lions tour to Australia, New Zealand and Papua New Guinea in 1984 and his try tally was 11 from 17 games, only one try behind the chart-topper, Ellery Hanley, who played the same number of games.

Des was not the only Drummond to play professional rugby league. His younger sibling, Alva, a wingman too, had many games at several clubs in Lancashire, but there was only one Des Drummond.

Of the many players I have had in my charge, Des had just about everything a wingman needed. His crash tackle, as described, would rate an 'H' (horror) certificate in the old cinemas and because of his second sport, judo, he possessed a hip throw, based on balance and timing, that allowed him to bring down the biggest of opponents. He served his clubs and his country with supreme honour and my hero didn't go out with a whimper either. On leaving his long-time club Leigh, he had several successful seasons at Warrington, starring for them in the 1986-87 Premiership Final, although Warrington lost 8-0 to Wigan. His final move to Workington Town brought him a runners'-up and winners' medal from the Second Division Premiership Final, losing to Featherstone Rovers in a tight game 20-16 and one year later, in 1994, Town beat London Crusaders to lift the title 30-22, and Des scored a beautiful try.

Des was a wonderful person to work with and a hero that I am proud to say that I coached him at the highest level.

	App	Tries	Goals	Pts
Leigh	278+2	141	2	470
Warrington	182	69	0	276
Workington	71	32	0	128
Lancashire	4	3	0	13
Great Britain	24	8	0	28
England	5	1	0	3

Brian Edgar

In the old days, to be selected for a Lions tour was a dream of every player who played in professional rugby league. Form seemed to improve for all in the few weeks prior to the selections being published in the hope of being one of the couple of surprise selections that always emerged when a touring side was picked.

If you were a good international player, one who had made a place your own, then there was a possibility that, if your personal form was good and if your club side was going well both in cup and league football, then maybe, just, maybe, you may make a second tour. Now that would be something, but what would the odds be of making three tours? As a forward, not many. There were more chances as a back, but from the first tour in 1910 through to 1966, two forwards made three tours, with the normal four years between each tour. Joe Thompson, the big Welshman who played at Leeds for many years was one; the other was the big, tough Cumbrian, Brian Edgar. Originally a second-rower, Brian made his first tour in 1958 when, as a rip-roaring forward from the iron-hard district of Workington, he was joined by his team-mates Harry Archer, Ike Southward and Bill Wookey. The strength of the Cumbrian and north western area's game in general at that time can be seen because besides the Workington players, fellow Cumbrians Dick Huddart of Whitehaven, Alvin Ackerley from Halifax and Barrow's Denis Goodwin and Phil Jackson joined them.

Brian Edgar and his Cumbrians had as a joint tour manager one of the great characters of the game from the north west, Tom Mitchell, the chairman of Workington Town, who was rumoured to work at times for MI5. Tom had known Brian since childhood and had been instrumental in securing his services for Town since he was 17-years-old, on a life contract.

The Lions' superb pack also included Alan Prescott, Tommy Harris, Brian McTigue, John Whiteley and Vince Karalius. The half-backs were Dave Bolton and Alex Murphy, with Mick Sullivan and Ike Southward on the flanks and the centres from Eric Ashton, Alan Davies or Phil Jackson. After Bolton's injury in the second test, Phil Jackson, at six-feet one-inch and 15 stones played stand-off in the third test, which Great Britain won and took the Ashes with a 40-17 victory. What wonderful days the likes of Brian Edgar gave us then.

The 1962 tour gave Great Britain the Ashes again with Brian operating in the second-row in all but one of the five tests. He missed the first Kiwi

Test in Auckland because of injury. And in 1966, with tour captain Harry Poole injured, Brian led the tourists in all three tests against Australia, but the Lions just failed to retain the Ashes, winning the first test 17-13, and losing the next two, by 6-4 and 19-14, a very close series indeed.

Brian was a player very much in the Brian McTigue mould, but quite a bit bigger than the Wigan forward. Edgar was a big bloke, tall and heavily set. He too was a 'stand-in-the-tackle' man, but could also break the line and in his second-row days was a match for any forward over 30 yards. His defence was uncompromising. In those days when Vince McKeating, John Henderson, Andy Key, Ces Thompson, Billy Iveson, the Australian John Mudge, Brian Edgar, Norman Herbert and Bill Martin played, the Cumbrian defences were things of utter pain and discomfort. No-one wanted to make that mind bending trip, usually in those days by train to Carlisle and a bus across the mountains, and then return after a good hiding from these big, strange forwards that Workington and Whitehaven were supposed to have found wandering around the fells.

That's what it felt like when going to the cold, cold north west, but besides being big, strong and fast, the forwards could all play too and in Brian Edgar they found a world class exponent. Touring three times was a marvellous achievement, but a forward of the class of Brian Edgar possibly threw away his chances of more club medals by staying true to his Workington commitment. I feel sure that he could have moved to St Helens, Wigan or Warrington had he wished and picked up many more Challenge Cup and Lancashire Cup medals than he could have hoped for at Derwent Park. But the big Cumbrian stayed at home for the whole of his wonderful career and between 1958 and 1966 picked up 11 Great Britain caps.

Just before he passed away, I was taking the Prescot 'A' team to play at Whitehaven and we stopped at the Tebay services for a cuppa. In the services were four great former players, travelling all the way up to Workington to see their ill mate Brian. Danny Gardner, Billy Boston and Colin Clarke from the Wigan area and the brilliant wingman Johnny Stopford of Swinton were all going to visit their hero, the great Brian Edgar.

	App	Tries	Goals	Pts
Workington Town	384	83	27	303
Cumberland	13	2	0	6
Great Britain	11	0	0	0

Don Ellis

Don Ellis may be a surprise inclusion in a book of heroes, but I played several seasons under Don when he coached the amateur team I played for when I left Dewsbury. This team was Burton Sports in the old Leeds and District League. A tough kid, Don had done his national service in the fight against Communism in Malaya, and like most in that campaign, had had it rough.

Two years of army life had given Don the edge when it came to training and fitness and although not the best footballing coach I played for, he certainly understood what was needed in the fitness and motivational side of the game. Because his running programmes were sickeningly tough, it became a challenge to me to complete whatever Don threw at us. I was a bit ancient by this time, but by being determined not to let him beat me, the hard regime made me fitter than I had ever been before. As well as being trainer and coach, Don was also the captain of the side which, I may add, without being a world-beating outfit, was a strong side in the highly competitive league.

The middle 1960s were particularly good years for us at Burton Sports with Leeds and District Cup wins in 1965 and 1966, a championship win in 1967 and a memorable amateur Yorkshire Cup run which took us to the final, played at Tattersfield, Doncaster's ground, only to lose to a very strong Hull Embassy side. That cup run included a magnificent semi-final win at the redoubtable Dewsbury Celtic, who were Yorkshire Cup kingpins then, but in a gale, and monsoon conditions, our much lighter side tackled heroically to pull off a superb win 5-4 with, as usual, Don Ellis leading from the front.

Standing six-feet three-inches and tipping the scales at over 15 stones, Don was a big lad. He had started playing at a late age compared to most of the side, and had joined Burton Sports as a tall, slim forward who played hard and tackled tough, but was just an ordinary run-of-the-mill back-rower until he left Burton Sports and went to play for his place of work, Bison concrete works in the Stourton area of Leeds. At Bison Sports, Don played with some good former professionals and benefited from a move to loose-forward at Bisons. His game changed from a head-down, bum-up, grafting type to an upright runner who was big enough to stand in the tackle and deliver some superb little passes that I particularly liked running off. His kicking game too suddenly blossomed and his ability to draw the opposition defence onto him and chip kick, with pin point accuracy into space, was a rare skill indeed.

His courageous leadership too was a huge plus on his playing CV and his outstanding presence on the field was the flag around which we rallied. Don represented Yorkshire and played well enough to gain an England amateur cap against the French. Another mark of his ability was that his selection for England defied the 'old club tie' system that governed policy in those times. Playing for your county, and even more for your country, depended a lot on which club you played for and which county you played in. Don was picked on ability.

He also dabbled in trials for a professional club and tells a great story about when, during the time he was playing for Bisons, the Keighley club asked him to play three trial games in the first team, with a view to signing him if he shaped up to the club's requirements. Don agreed, trained at Lawkholme Lane, now Cougar Park, and duly played his three games, which happened to be Leeds, away, and two stiff games at home. Having a blinder at Leeds and scoring a good try in the bargain, Don then produced two excellent games in front of the Keighley fans.

The supporters loved his all-out, tough tackling style and after the three trials, Don approached the club chairman, Mr Smallwood, to ask if they intended to sign him. "We would like you to play another three Don, because we just want another look at you," he said, as most chairmen did then. Don was disappointed and said, "But I had three outstanding games, and I thought that would be enough". Mr Smallwood smiled and replied, "Ah yes Don, you did, but three fine days don't make a summer".

Keighley made a big mistake because Don Ellis would have made an excellent professional forward, take my word on that. But the professional game's loss was the amateurs' gain and big Don went on for many, many years and, like wine, got better with age. He returned to Burton Sports, was a terrific player to play alongside and had an outstanding advantage in that his players trusted him to be there for them on the field; he never let them down.

A strong disciplinarian on the field, Don led from the front and expected all others to do the same. His personality kept me in the amateur game for many years after my professional period as player. I copied Don's training techniques in my professional coaching career because he was a hero.

	App	Tries	Goals	Pts
Keighley	3	1	0	3

Also played for Burton Sports, Bison Sports, Yorkshire (amateurs), England (amateurs).

Andy Farrell OBE

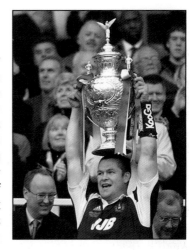

It is hard to find anything new to say about Andy Farrell. Although he has been around now for more than 10 years, he has that aura around him that makes you think he is still the fresh-faced kid in his teens who came along in 1993 and smashed his way into the big time, big style. For all his fame and fortune, Andy seems to have found that secret of maintaining his feet on the ground that only a few youngsters find if success comes thick and fast while still learning this game of ours.

I say this because only once have I been in the same company as him and he came out of his way to say hello and have a short discussion about the game. He was very polite indeed about my career and he spoke with common sense about the Wigan club and the game in general, again showing great maturity for someone so young at that time. Always a big lad, Andy shot into the frame when, in his first full season, he was a playing substitute in the Wembley Challenge Cup Final of May 1993 when Wigan beat Phil Larder's Widnes 20-14. In early November of the same year, the young Farrell made a try-scoring debut for Great Britain at Headingley, in a 29-10 victory against France.

True to the Central Park tradition, the Wigan club had six players on duty that day and five in the second game of that series in March 1994, when Andy kicked his first goal for his country in a 12-4 win in Carcassonne. His pedigree in the game was honed and sharpened within the highly competitive set-up at firstly, Central Park, then at the brand new JJB stadium in Wigan. Joining the club as an youngster, Andy followed the endless list of local lads who came from the Wigan area and reached the highest levels of the game in gaining many cup and trophy winners' medals and representing Great Britain.

But Andy went one further than that; he has captained his country against all the major test playing nations. This again shows the calibre of the man; he became skipper as a young player and never lost the job from day one. In his early days he had a good platform from which to study some great players, as his team mates included Dean Bell, Andy Platt, Denis Betts, Kelvin Skerrett, Phil Clarke, Jason Robinson, Martin Dermott, Shaun Edwards, Martin Offiah and Frano Botica. In fact the whole squad was filled with top, skilful players.

Andy's commitment to his club and his team mates was seen in a hard fought and very close game on television. In one horrendous clash Andy reeled away with a gashed and broken nose. He was led away to the dressing rooms to be stitched up and treated and no-one considered that he would return, so bad was the injury. The result looked to be going away from Wigan but out of the dressing rooms, with his damaged nose and cheekbones covered in what appeared to be a *Phantom of the Opera* mask, came, amid tumultuous cheering from the Wigan fans, one Andy Farrell. With a fearless attitude, and no thought to the heavily bandaged broken nose, he led his troops from the front and gained a historic victory. The rapturous applause as he left the arena told all. He was the hero of the hour.

In our game there have been many acts of heroism, such as the 'Rorke's Drift' test on the 1914 Lions tour when the Lions were reduced to 10 men, then nine for a spell, but held out to win the test match, and the Lions captain Alan Prescott, playing with a broken arm in the Brisbane test in 1958 and leading his team to a great victory that enabled them to win the series. This act by Andy Farrell was not in a test match, but it was for his club, Wigan, and to play for Wigan is tantamount to playing for your country, so strong is the tradition at the club.

Andy Farrell has been an excellent example for all youngsters to follow, one club, one country and will move heaven and earth for both. His natural gift to be able to break defences and score those game-breaking tries, plus his ability to kick long-range and touchline conversions, seem to be motivated by his determination to win for the cherry and whites and he continued to perform at the highest level with a consistency that is unbelievable.

His contribution was not as dramatic for Great Britain and we saw him in a different guise when in red, white and blue. Here he took the role of grafter or workhorse, one who led with hard work and the spectacular stuff comes from others and this, I think, is the beauty of Andy Farrell. His game is of three faces: his Wigan one where his play against the club sides is outstanding, and his international one of unselfish toil. His third face is as yet unseen, that of playmaker in international rugby union as Farrell joins his former Wigan and Great Britain team mate Jason Robinson in the XV-a-side code's England set up. No matter which code Farrell plays, he will be heroic.

	App	Tries	Goals	Pts
Wigan	348+21	111	1,355	3,135
Lancashire	3	0	10	20
England	11	3	33	78
Great Britain	33	4	53	122

Tony Fisher

Tony is without doubt one of the toughest men to play rugby league in the post war period. Tony's elder brother Idwal was playing at Odsal and Tony fancied his chances at the XIII-a-side game even though he was brought up playing union in Wales. He was in the RAF at the time and was a boxing champion. On his demob he signed for Northern and so started the career of a legend.

He was such a strong man and, while not of a giant build, was, as they say, big enough! He was from that breed of men who had learned their hooking trade in a hard school. In Tony's time, and indeed from the first time any form of rugby football was played, the position of hooker was no place for faint hearts. The broken noses and cauliflower ears were badges of courage, the scar tissue around the eyes told of many a battle, sometimes won, sometimes lost, but win or lose the hooker, of all the forwards, had to come up to scratch at the bell. Thus began the mythology of the hooker. Usually great company with a sense of humour second to none, they were the life-and-soul of the team, and first in if any of his mates was in trouble.

Tony Fisher was the classical pre-Super League hooker. Word went around that Bradford Northern had brought a hard case to the club from Wales and teams quickly realised how true that was as Tony's reputation preceded him. The combinations of front-row forwards that included Tony were awesome. Playing for Wales, Tony was the middle man between Jim Mills and Bobby Wanbon, with John Mantle too sometimes moving forward from the second-row, to make up a tremendously tough trio.

However, it was at Great Britain level that Tony excelled. Selected for the 1970 tour he joined a band of players who have gone down in the game's history as the last team to win the Ashes from the Australians, home or away. The front row of Dennis Hartley, Tony and Cliff Watson laid a fantastic foundation for the test wins and added to the belief among many former test players that to beat the Australians victory must start in the front-row.

The touring Lions of 1970 was just about the best balanced side to ever leave these shores, and the front row put the fear of God up the Australians. To be fair, the Australians won the first test 37-15, and the strange thing was that in the second test the Australians left out three of their winning forwards from that first test, one of whom, blind-side prop Morgan, had scored two tries. Great Britain's front row in that first test was Dave Chisnall, Peter Flanagan and Cliff Watson, a good set, but not as strong and aggressive as the alternative with Hartley and Fisher in it.

Tony scored a try in the second test in a 28-7 win and in the decider in Sydney, big Dennis Hartley scored his historic try in the pulsating 21-17 win to secure the Ashes.

Tony Fisher played in four of the six tests against Australia and New Zealand and was a vital piece in the successful selection jigsaw on tour.

Tony had two spells at Odsal, between stints at Leeds and Castleford and, in all, collected 11 Great Britain caps, as well as 14 caps for Wales, including appearing in the 1970 European Championship.

One of his claims to even more fame followed his selection on Guy Fawkes Day 1978, against the Australian tourists, when the Great Britain coach, Peter Fox, picked what was called the 'Dads' Army' team, with a front-row of Jim Mills, Tony Fisher and Brian Lockwood, all considered to past their best. Down, one test to nil, and needing to win this one at Odsal to keep the series alive, the Dads' Army took the Australians to the cleaners, and although the score was close at 18-14, the British team stormed to a series-saving win, with all to play for in the final test at Headingley on 18 November. This time the dream failed and Great Britain went down heavily, 23-6. It was Tony's last test as a new era of hookers was emerging.

But Tony, forever the enthusiast, went into coaching and did a good job wherever he worked, including at Bramley, Keighley and Doncaster. We coached against each other on several occasions but my lasting memory of Tony comes from 7 November 1970 when Great Britain were beaten in the World Cup Final by Australia. It was a tight game, 12-7 in the Australians' favour at the end, and this no-holds-barred game suddenly erupted into a mass brawl, with Tony fighting the Australians' biggest forward, John 'Lurch' O'Neill. Tony won as all his boxing skills came to the fore and his hard punches had the big New South Welshman out for the count in short time.

A Great Britain test hero: Tony Fisher.

	App	Tries	Goals	Pts
Bradford Northern	76+1	2	0	6
Leeds	121+20	10	1	32
Castleford	47	1	0	3
Great Britain	11	0	0	0
Wales	16	1	0	3

Neil Fox MBE

The fabulous Neil Fox is so unassuming that he may well be embarrassed if he heard anyone call him that, but he was terrific. The younger brother of Peter and Don, Neil formed a trio who became legends in the game of rugby league - Neil and Don as wonderful international players and Peter as a professional player of many seasons, but more widely known as a coach of great standing and a Yorkshire and Great Britain boss.

I first saw Neil as a newly signed youngster when, as a player for Hull FC I played against a Wakefield Trinity 'A' team that included a big young centre with a prodigious left-footed kick. I recall that a try against us in the final seconds of the game took Trinity to within a point of our score and because the try was scored by the corner flag, the conversion would have to be from the touchline to beat us. Up came this strapping youngster and, from the wrong side for him, he belted the ball over the bar for the winning points. That was one of Neil's many skills, and he employed those skills for years, not only in Great Britain, but all over the rugby league playing world.

The club at which he found fame was grand old Wakefield Trinity, the leading Yorkshire club for long spells in the late 1950s and throughout the 1960s, and Neil's pairing in the centres with that classical player, South African Alan Skene, was untouchable. Comparable to a broadsword and a rapier, Fox and Skene complemented each other perfectly and when Alan Skene returned home, Neil found another equally mobile partner in the quicksilver Ian Brooke.

Neil Fox was a massive centre, not only tall but strong and because of his physique spectators, mostly those of other clubs, who wished with all their heart that Neil was playing for them, thought that the big man lacked that yard of pace. I say garbage to that. Study the number of long-range tries he scored and then say he lacked a yard - not in a million years. His great career achievements are testimony to his brilliant ability.

To say that he was a Fox brother is enough to anyone lucky enough to remember the three players to realise what a good football brain he possessed. Neil famously showed this ability in a match playing for Hull Kingston Rovers towards the end of his career. In a tight game Rovers were awarded a penalty kick. Quick as a flash, Neil seized the ball and, as the team's goalkicker, dug his heel in the ground, whispered to the referee: "I'm going to tap the ball, sir", while at the same time pointing at the posts, intimating a kick at goal. The opposition relaxed, turned their backs on Neil and began organising catchers, just in case the ball hit the posts and came out. Neil took a quick tap and was over the line to score the winning try. Perfectly fair and above board, he simply outsmarted the opposition. However, the smart Fox move was seen soon after as a loophole in the laws of the game and that is why, today, the referee has to send his touch-judges behind the goal when a player is taking a penalty shot at goal, to signal a successful kick or not, but also to allow the defensive side time to adjust. All that was thanks to the wily Fox.

Neil toured with the Lions of 1962, under the captaincy of Eric Ashton, and played in all the tests on that successful Ashes tour, scoring 19 tries and kicking 85 goals on the trip. His 574 games for Wakefield Trinity are second only to Harry Wilkinson's 605 and no one on that fabulous club's records can match his 1,836 goals or his 272 tries, a total of 4,488 points. Other first class games gave Neil a wonderful total of 2,575 goals, 358 tries and 6,220 points in his career, a world record for points-scoring, and also puts him as one of only three players to kick 300 goals and score 300 tries in their careers, the other two being Eric Ashton for Wigan and Ike Southward for Workington Town and Oldham, before Super League.

But I remember Neil Fox for other, more personal reasons, like the time I was assistant coach to his brother Peter at Bramley. Peter was also the Great Britain coach at the same time and was on international duty on the day the club had to go up to Workington in a league game. I was a novice compared to the side I took over for Peter, but Neil, who was playing for Bramley that day, stood in the dressing room and said: "Listen, we will support Maurice today, do as he says and work to what he wants, now let's listen to him". It was a great statement from a legend, a wonderful player, a gentleman and a hero.

	App	Tries	Goals	Pts
Wakefield Trinity	562+12	272	1,836	4,488
Bradford Northern	57+13	12	86	205
Hull KR	59	16	214	470
York	12+1	2	42	90
Bramley	23	6	73	164
Huddersfield	21	5	74	160
Yorkshire	17	9	60	147
Great Britain	29	12	93	222
England	1	1	3	9

Tony Garforth

Talk about respect with hard men. They all respected Tony Garforth. He was, and is, a quiet bloke. Always prepared to greet you with a smile, and always nice to chat with no matter how long between meetings. He was also a cracking prop forward, not of international standard but certainly county class. His presence was a fillip to whichever team he played for, as he would lift the side with a big tackle or a powerful burst just when you needed it.

I must go back in my coaching career to remember my first meeting with Tony. It was at the old Crown Flatt ground in Dewsbury, and I was the assistant coach taking training one night when a committeeman came onto the training area accompanied by a finely built young man in his training gear. I was introduced to Tony. He had been recommended by our club scout and I knew that he was a hot property as I had already heard about this tough forward. Tony wanted to have a look around the club and train with us prior to talking about the business of signing. He talked to the committee, but the club could not match the excellent terms offered by Wakefield Trinity, but watching him train and meeting and talking to him made a big impression on me and would help me in the not too distant future. To say that Tony would look for any sort of trouble would be wrong. To say he would do his best to avoid trouble, but if unable to do so would meet that trouble head on, hence a reputation away from rugby, as a hard case - not a make-believe world of the cinema but a fact as seen by many.

One Sunday lunchtime in his local pub, Tony was put in a corner by a well known fighting man with a big reputation. The hard case wanted to give Tony a going over. In the no-win situation Tony set about the bully and ended the argument quickly. The action was seen by one of my junior players who couldn't wait to tell me about it on the following Tuesday evening. "You know Tony Garforth don't you, Maurice?" the kid asked me. I said that I did and because I knew him, I became as big a hero as Tony to the young player.

People said to me "You won't be able to handle him" when I signed him at Halifax in 1979, but I knew my man and also knew that if treated correctly no-one would have any trouble from Tony. I had to wait some five years to get my tough prop. We were building up a strong squad at Halifax in an attempt to get promotion after narrowly missing out the season before and Tony was just the forward I wanted. I signed him from Keighley and he enjoyed himself from day one. He was a protective figure to all the players on the field. No one took liberties with any of my players when Tony was about and his toughness and playing ability were a big plus to our promotion hopes.

Never out of the first team squad, Tony's adaptability proved a great help in securing promotion because if he came off the bench, he could be used in so many ways, as a power runner or to bolster up the defence with his tough tackling. He was a dream signing and another big plus was that the other players rated him highly. The spectators at Halifax liked him too because he was a throwback to the old fashioned type of forward that had become synonymous with Thrum Hall - no nonsense, hard and uncompromising. That was his strength and like so many tough players he never moaned if hurt. And he seemed to know if the incident had been an accident or intended. If accidental, he let it go, but if intentional, then look out.

He was not a dirty player and he despised any form of liberty taking. He played hard and would target dangerous players with hard but perfectly fair tackles. Three seasons later I was coaching Bramley and within a week I had signed two players I thought would lift the club, hooker Peter Clarke and Tony Garforth. Both came at the back end of their careers, but Tony stayed on for several seasons at the old McLaren Field and must have been one of the club's most loyal and worthwhile bargain buys. To Garforth and Clarke I added Alan Hindley, another tough prop from a Leigh junior club and later brought in big George Ballentyne from Castleford, giving us one of the best front rows in the Second Division, but the main man was Tony. He always gave 100 per cent, and did the same job for me at Bramley as he had at Halifax. He looked after the young and not-so-young too and was a fine player.

While playing at Rochdale for Bramley, Tony was kicked on the forehead by a stray boot by a renowned kicker and hacker. With several stitches, like a zip, straight down his head, Tony approached the opposition player after the game and asked if it was intentional or not. The man knew Tony and immediately apologised and assured Tony that it was an accident. Perhaps this was a clever move: considering the stitches, but Tony wanted to know. What a hero!

	App	Tries	Goals	Pts
Wakefield Trinity	11+4	2	0	6
Keighley	119+4	16	0	48
Halifax	67+7	2	0	6
Bramley	86+3	9	0	29

Reg Gasnier

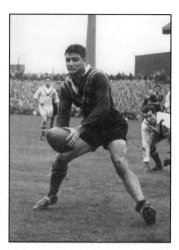

Australia has had its share of rugby league heroes. Some people imagine that before the upsurge of successful test wins by the Australians over the past 30 or so years that Britain had who won every time we played them before then. This is not the case. Although Australia now lead in the total of tests won, this record was only achieved recently, but the Australians have always produced brilliant individual players.

Reg Gasnier is one of those players. Possessing lightening speed and evasive qualities, he burst on the scene when selected in the trans-Tasman tests of 1959 where he played all three tests, and linked, for the first time with the redoubtable Harry Wells in the centres. Gasnier and Wells, the names brought gasps of astonishment and fear from opposing teams. Gasnier, at five-feet 11-inches and just over 12 stones was the flying machine, a 'ghost' in green and gold. Wells, six feet and around 15 stones, all power and vastly experienced, was a rampaging brick wall, who would dash at an opening and smash through it. As Wells created a yawning gap, who should suddenly appear on his shoulder, but Gasnier, running like the wind into the clear and over the tryline. It was superb stuff to which Britain had little answer.

The ideal centre partnership I was brought up with as a kid was a strong player and a speedy player. The one that the Australians came up with was the original combination. On occasion Wells acted as the perfect foil for Gasnier's pace because he would give the impression that he would take a pass, all pumped up aggression and demanding at least two tacklers to stop him, then the pass would miss him and find Gasnier, looping around on an arc, and through the slimmest of gaps caused by the dummy run of Wells. The perfect understanding between the pair was seen at its best on the Kangaroo tour of 1959 when, on his debut against Great Britain, Gasnier scored a brilliant hat-trick of tries in the first test at Swinton - a fantastic Australian 22-14 win. Although Gasnier was a totally self-reliant player who could win a match on his own, Wells's power and experience had a hand in creating all three tries. One came from a strong Wells burst through which Gasnier supported to stride over, and another from a close in hustle-and-bustle when Wells scattered three tacklers to hand a walk-in try to Reg, who was on hand to take the final pass. The third was pure Gasnier magic after Wells had used his dummy run to allow Reg to go in from the half-way line.

Another player who benefited from Gasnier's brilliance was his wing partner at St George, as well as for Australia, Eddie Lumsden. The pair were vital cogs in the wonderful record that St George established when the club won 11 straight Sydney Grand Finals, from 1956 to 1966. Although Reg played in the majority, he had to give way to Eddie Lumsden who holds the record for the Australian player with most Grand Final appearances.

Interestingly, Reg's historical partner, Wells, whose club football at home was played for South Sydney and Western Suburbs, was instrumental in bringing a British legend into the international game in that test in which Reg scored his hat-trick. To stop the threat of Wells in the centres, Great Britain gave a debut to a centre who was as big, if not bigger than Wells and the player whose presence allowed us to win both the second and third tests and retain the Ashes: Neil Fox.

Reg Gasnier toured three times in all, 1959, 1963 and 1967 along with another three-time tourist, the fabulous Johnny Raper and, although restricted to only five games on the 1967 tour because of injury, Reg played in a total of 27 tour games and scored 26 tries. His full total of international caps was 36, including two appearances against South Africa in 1963.

A superb, old-fashioned centre, yet with a modern ability to score the type of tries seen today. The old-fashioned part of his game was the way in which he made tries for his wing partner Eddie Lumsden. Reg had few weaknesses and fewer peers in his era. When conversations in Australian leagues clubs over a 'midi' or two turn to their great players and centres, two names crop up: H. H. Dally Messenger and Reg Gasnier. Both are genuine legends of the Australian game. The latter's name is synonymous, not only with Australia and New South Wales, but also with the St George club, the only Sydney team he played for. His nephew, Mark Gasnier, has maintained the family record as he played for Australia, New South Wales in State of Origin and for St George. He too is a cracking centre, much bigger than uncle Reg in physique, but he will have a long way to go to better his dad's brother on the meadow. Reg Gasnier, a larger than life hero.

	App	Tries	Goals	Pts
St George	129	127	20	421
New South Wales	16	13	3	45
Australia	36	26	0	78

Herbert Goodfellow

A player who represented the 'enemy' when I was a youngster was the superb scrum-half, technician and wonderful player, Herbert Goodfellow. Herbert proudly wore the blue and red of Wakefield Trinity when, immediately after the Second World War, I became a fanatical Leeds rugby league supporter. We all regarded Wakefield Trinity as the enemy.

I can picture him now, dark hair parted down the centre in the fashion of the day, small and slim, again as the scrum-half was in those days, but strong and with an easily recognized running style that looked as if he was falling forward, head first. Wakefield Trinity had a great reputation of producing half-backs, the legendary Jonty Parkin, still talked about over a pint in the Wakefield pubs, was the most famous after he went on three Lions tours, two as captain, but Herbert ranks a very close second as Trinity's all-time great number seven.

The little mining village of Sharlston, severely decimated in the closure of the Yorkshire coalfields in the 1980s, has produced a myriad of great rugby league players: the three Fox brothers, Jonty Parkin and Herbert Goodfellow to name but five. The village is still turning out tremendous amateur players to this day.

Herbert started his career at Sharlston School as a stand-off and achieved the ultimate accolade when chosen for Yorkshire Schoolboys against their Lancashire counterparts. A "good 'un" many said of the young Goodfellow, "but he's not going to be big enough for the pros". Leaving school at 14, he went, like the vast majority of lads in Sharlston, to work down the pit and, small or not, was signed by Trinity in 1932. He weighed only eight-and-a-half stones and was ensconced in the 'A' team for a full season to learn his trade. His first team debut, against Keighley came in 1933, when Herbert was only 16 years old and he was pitted against the strong and very experienced Ted Spillane, a Kiwi who joined Wigan in 1924 and later coached for many years at the Bramley club.

What a debut it was, for the slightly built junior scorched over for two tries and this adult display, plus the man's consistently great work behind the pack, ensured him selection as scrum-half for the next 20 years. In these years, Herbert developed from the small, slim boy into a very strong man, with an upper-body strength that caught the unaware opponent completely off guard. His guile and general know-how as a craftsman of the art of scrum-half play was a pleasure to behold. Herbert's tussles with the best half-backs in the world at the time, Tommy McCue, Dai Jenkins, Tommy Bradshaw, Donald Ward and Watkins, were worth the admission fee themselves. His work with his Trinity loose-forward partner, Len Bratley, was a masterful combination for many seasons. Herbert's strength of character can be seen when, after suffering thrombosis, he resumed playing, against medical advice, to once again entertain the Wakefield supporters with tremendous displays.

Among the many memorable games he played, the one against Leeds in September 1945 must stand out. Trinity in that game inflicted the heaviest defeat in the Leeds club's history with a 71-0 trouncing at Belle Vue. Another thriller was the Challenge Cup semi-final at Headingley in 1946, when Trinity beat Hunslet 7-3, Herbert making the crucial try for wingman Denis Baddeley. In this pulsating game O'Neill, the flying schoolmaster wingman for Hunslet, chased a kick through by team-mate Frank Watson, picked up and ran a good 60 yards seemingly to score the winner by the posts, but a touch judge flagged for offside and the score was denied. The flag waver was attacked by an irate Hunslet fan and suffered a broken jaw while the fan did six months inside for his crime.

Herbert gained a Challenge Cup winner's medal with the Wembley victory over Wigan that season and a Yorkshire Cup winner's medal in 1947-48 beating Leeds 8-7 at Odsal in a replay, after a 7-7 draw at Fartown. Herbert's only England cap was against Wales at Odsal in 1939 and it remains one of the biggest injustices that he was not capped for Great Britain. Five caps for Yorkshire, and being captain for his county, was his reward for being a top player for two decades.

His career at Wakefield encompassed 426 games, kicking 12 goals and scoring 115 tries, and ended in 1951 when he moved to Lancashire to play for Oldham where he finished his illustrious career. Would he have been as good today? I would like to think so because he had a full repertoire of skills, was strong, brave and quick enough to trouble most defences. Above all, Herbert gained a great reputation because he symbolised the good things that came with our game then: bravery and heroism, enough said.

	App	Tries	Goals	Pts
Wakefield Trinity	426	115	12	369
Oldham	23	2	0	6
Yorkshire	5	0	0	0
England	1	0	0	0

Jeff Grayshon MBE

Born in Birstall, between Batley, Bradford and Leeds, Jeff played association football as a youngster, but was invited up to the old Crown Flatt ground to have a run with the 'A' team at Dewsbury. Tall and slim in those days, Jeff was thought to have the makings of a good full-back and actually played in that position when he was signed. An astute committeeman noted Jeff's hard tackling and strong running and he was asked to try out in the second-row. He liked the rough and tumble of the forwards better than the long periods of inactivity at full-back and made a very mobile duo with fellow second-rower, future international and touring Lion, John Bates.

Jeff's early promise began to mature in the 1972-73 season when the Dewsbury side as a whole, coached by the astute former Featherstone Rovers loose-forward, Tommy Smales, became a force within the game and, out of the blue, reached the Yorkshire Cup Final, to be beaten 36-9 by Leeds, then the Championship Final, this time beating Leeds 22-13. Jeff's form in that successful season earmarked him as a future international and, as his experience grew, so did his reputation. His size increased too and in the place of that young, slim full-back, now stood a big man, weighing in at around 16 stones.

He had a spell playing in Australia at Cronulla-Sutherland and during this period suffered a severe knee injury that required a reconstruction of the joint. On his return to Dewsbury, he was offered the player-coach job, in an effort to lift the flagging club, but a lifeline to his playing career was thrown to him by the Bradford Northern coach, Peter Fox, and in 1978 off Jeff went to Odsal.

Jeff, like quite a few good players, never found his way to a Wembley Challenge Cup Final. Lots of winning medals in other cup competitions came his way, but the cherished trip to the twin towers never materialised. Jeff made 13 Great Britain appearances and was a Lion on the 1979 tour of Australia and New Zealand where he played in five of the six test matches. He played 10 times for England and 14 for Yorkshire.

The first time I worked with Jeff was in 1972 when I accepted the assistant coach's job at Dewsbury. Jeff had just made the place in the Crown Flatt pack his own and was playing really well. On the few occasions he turned out, after first-team injury, with my 'A' team, he played just as hard for me as he did for Great Britain years later. This was always a good measurement of a player's enthusiasm, because I have had one or two first-team players who didn't care about playing in the 'A' team. Jeff always gave 100 per cent.

In 1985 I was coaching Great Britain and was in a quandary over selecting a side for the crucial second test against New Zealand at Wigan. Without going too deeply into our national weaknesses, at that time we had a huge shortage of prop forwards. Kevin Ward, who later returned for me, was in self-imposed exile from the Great Britain set-up, Lee Crooks was injured and we had to win to stay in the series. It was vital to the game in this country that we made some sort of show against the Kiwis who had beaten us soundly in three straight test matches the year before.

We had lost the first test 24-22, after appearing to have it won, so success in the Wigan test was as much a saviour for the game in Great Britain as any played before in its history. Enter Jeff Grayshon, who had been selected before for Great Britain by Peter Fox, then the coach at Leeds, as we prepared at the Shaw Hill complex at Chorley. The week before I had phoned Jeff at home and simply asked my old friend if he could, at the ripe young age of 37 years, "do a job for his country, and me!" "With pleasure Maurice," he answered. So Jeff became the oldest player ever to represent Great Britain in test football. By the way, his presence in the camp, in the dressing room and on the field of play helped us considerably and we won that vital test 25-8.

Jeff had another great game for his country in the third and final test at Elland Road when, in a game remembered for Lee Crooks' prodigious last minute penalty goal, we ground out a 6-6 draw that also drew the series and put us back on the long road to respectability.

Jeff moved to Featherstone with Peter Fox then back home to Batley to coach at Mount Pleasant to round off a memorable career before being awarded the MBE in June 1992.

While at Featherstone, Jeff created another first when he played against his son, Paul, who played for Bradford. Paul tackled Jeff and left him over the touchline, gasping for breath. A wag in the crowd called out: "If I were you Jeff, I'd smack his arse and send him to bed!" Jeff laughed as much as anyone at the remark.

My final memory of Jeff is the job he did for me just prior to the Kiwi test when he helped Great Britain win the Presidents Trophy in Limoux, France, and quietened the wild French prop, Max Chantel in good style. But you wouldn't expect any less from a great big hero, Jeff Grayshon.

	App	Tries	Goals	Pts
Dewsbury	235+2	31	2	96
Cronulla	7	0	0	0
Bradford Northern	244+11	37	0	119
Leeds	31+2	1	0	4
Featherstone	97+3	2	0	8
Batley	69+35	2	0	8
Yorkshire	14	0	0	0
England	9+1	1	0	3
Great Britain	13	1	0	3

Eric Grothe

Like most of the 1982 Invincibles, the first Australian touring side to complete a tour unbeaten, Eric Grothe was virtually an unknown quantity. Hardly anyone in Britain had heard of Mal Meninga, Brett Kenny, Peter Sterling, Wayne Pearce, Steve Ella, Gene Miles, Wally Lewis or Eric Grothe. We were soon to find out about them all. But I was lucky to work with Eric for a short while when he came over to play for Leeds when I was in my first spell as coach there.

I had seen him play for Australia live and on video, and was amazed at his ability to run so powerfully and speedily when in what seemed almost a crouched position. It was all down to his low centre of gravity, or so the experts told me, what that is in reality I never have been able to work out. Well over 6 feet tall and tipping the scales at 14 stones, Eric was a big, strong lad. In his debut for Leeds at Headingley, Eric asked if he could play on the right wing instead of the left and I agreed. By all accounts he preferred the right, but politics in Australia demanded that Kerry Boustead played there and so Eric had filled the left wing berth.

The game was against Leigh and we won comfortably with Eric scoring three tries. On one rampaging run for a score, the tough and very mobile Leigh second-rower, Tony Cottrell, charged across in a cover tackle, attempting to stop Eric, but was greeted with a steam-hammer hand off that hit Tony flush in the chest. He dropped like a stone and Eric went on to register a 40-yard try. Milton Novis was the Leeds club doctor and he was off his seat and onto the field in record in record time as he had seen how Tony had fallen and was concerned. Doc Novis told me later that Tony's heart had stopped, momentarily, and the good doctor revived him immediately. Such was the power of Eric Grothe.

His record at Leeds was 14 tries in 16 matches, a remarkable achievement. But it is his defensive qualities that I remember as well as his athletic try scoring. In one game at Oldham, with Leeds hanging on to an 8-8 draw going into injury time, Oldham's speedy wingman, Mick Taylor, intercepted a wayward Leeds pass almost on his own line and, running down the famous Watersheddings slope, looked certain to win the game for his side in the final seconds. I swear that I heard Eric Grothe, chasing across the field from the opposite wing. The thud, thud, thud of his feet could be heard above the cheering Oldham faithful. Only inches from the tryline Eric hurled his huge frame at the unfortunate Taylor and knocked down the flying wingman and the corner flag, with a memorable, match-saving tackle.

Eric played in eight Tests for Australia and scored 10 tries for his country. A very quiet man, he would join in celebrations with his team-mates, but preferred to sit at the back of the bus on long trips to away matches, playing his guitar, which he did expertly. He was, in those days, a bit of a hippie, with his long hair, laid-back lifestyle and attitude.

I have gone on record before saying that Eric was just about the worst player I ever had to train, but he was also the best wingman I had the luck to work with. Even the hard-to-please Leigh, Warrington and Workington wing star, Des Drummond, another great wingman, begrudgingly said: "Yeah, Grothe is a good 'un".

Another great story about Eric comes from that Australian 1982 ultra successful tour. Playing at Headingley against Leeds, the Australians had rattled up a big score and David Ward the outstanding Leeds captain was asked, by John Holmes the superb Leeds stand-off, late in the game to whom he should kick a drop-out to. David looked about him and said: "Kick the bloody thing as far away from our line as you can, kick it to that bloke with the long hair!" David Ward said, indicating towards Eric Grothe. You will recall the Australians were largely unknown on these shores.

We now know that Holmes should have kicked it to anyone but Eric. Grothe caught the kick and promptly ran back to the Leeds posts to score, after skittling several Leeds tacklers on the way to a 50-yard try.

Eric is a family man and on his short spell at Leeds brought over his wife and two small boys. The oldest of his children, Eric jnr, now stars for Parramatta on the wing, just like his dad.

Eric's exploits for his only club side, Paramatta, are legend and he was a member of four Grand Final winning teams. A regular in the New South Wales State of Origin side and a true gentleman both on and off the field, Eric Grothe, like most Australians was given a nickname which still lasts to this day - 'the Guru' - obviously from his days as a hippie. He guarded his privacy vehemently, but where his football was concerned, approached it with a smile, and very professionally indeed. One all time great wingman and a nice bloke, the Guru.

	App	Tries	Goals	Pts
Parramatta	143+7	78	0	284
Leeds	16	14	0	56
New South Wales	9	3	0	10
Australia	8	10	0	34

Bob Haigh

Bob was, and indeed still is, one of nature's gentlemen. Lovely man that he is, his gentleness masks a hard centre as his record as a back-row forward in the toughest of games proves. A Wakefield lad, his junior rugby was played at Crigglestone School, then onto Trinity's junior and intermediate teams before finally signing for his home town team in 1962.

They did things right at Wakefield then and Bob was signed to be groomed to take over from Derek Turner when the master loose-forward called it a day. The Trinity pack then boasted four full internationals and two county forwards and although introduced early and given a taste of the big time, Bob was not rushed into first-team football. In 1963 he was a regular in the first team but following a re-jig of the side in 1964 he moved into the second-row and found his niche to become one of the best second-rowers of his era.

By 1967 Bob had several medals to his credit, including a League Championship winner's medal plus selection that year for the England under-23 side to play France in Bayonne. A tremendous runner, Bob developed into a prolific try scorer and when superb ballplayer, Don Fox, signed at Belle Vue, Bob found himself more and more in try-scoring mode. As Bob made his name as a try-scorer, he was already rated as the best cover tackler in the game. Cover tackling was a skill, usually of back-row forwards, who would cover across the back of their advancing line of defence and tackle any of the opposition who broke that line. The classic sight of a wingman being put into the clear and a covering forward scything him down with a perfect leg tackle into touch is typical of Bob's defensive work.

Bob played in the traumatic 'Watersplash' Challenge Cup Final of 1968, the game remembered for the last minute conversion miss by the unlucky Don Fox. Bob did take something from that season though as he gained selection for the 1968 World Cup squad for the tournament in Australia and New Zealand. The following year he made his first, and try scoring, appearance for Yorkshire against Cumberland at Hull Kingston Rovers' Craven Park and the following month scored tries for England against Wales at Leeds and then against France at Wigan. Bob's Great Britain career covered five full caps and one substitute's role. His final cap was in 1971 against the Kiwis.

Bob just missed out on selection for the 1970 Lions tour but after 250 games and 58 tries for Trinity, he moved the few miles from Belle Vue to Headingley in April 1970 for the princely sum of £6,000, a record fee for Trinity.

The likeable Bob Haigh was soon wowing the Leeds fans with his blockbuster power running and superb cover defending. Bob's feeding off the prompting of Don Fox at Wakefield was continued in similar style at Headingley, when he formed a formidable partnership with the ball-handling magician, Ray Batten, the Leeds loose-forward. Batten's role in the duet was to hit the defensive line, Haigh then appeared at full speed, Batten slipped the ball into the path of the rampaging second-rower and it was all over: a try! In the 1970-71 season, Bob recorded an unbelievable 40 tries for Leeds; which smashed the then 45-year-old former record held by the old Hull FC favourite, Bob Taylor, who had 36. Supporters swear that 39 of Bob's tries came from Ray Batten's deft handling. It was a wonderful effort and Bob to this day is generous in his thanks to the part played by Batten. Bob moved on from Leeds to Bradford Northern in the 1976-77 season and after playing in the same team at Wakefield with the great Fox brothers, Neil and Don, he joined their elder brother, Peter, at Odsal and under his coaching gained many successes.

In the 1979-80 season, I was coaching at Halifax and heard that Bob was considering a move to Dewsbury along with two players I had coached both at Bramley and at Odsal with Peter Fox: Jack Austin and Johnny Wolford. My football chairman, Ron Dobson, and I went to see Bob at his home with the intension of signing him, but unfortunately he had signed at Crown Flatt that afternoon. Bob played in·the semi-final of the Yorkshire Cup against us that season in a game that we won 5-3 and was the first to congratulate us at the final whistle, a gentleman to the end. A few years later I did sign Haigh, not Bob, but his son Mark who signed for me at Dewsbury and played for 10 years at the club, earning a very well-deserved benefit.

Bob Haigh was another player one would pay to watch because he always produced that important ingredient – excitement. His balanced running brought crowds to their feet and his defence caused a tingle down the spine. He was a truly worthy international who never forgot his background and was always a hero and gentleman.

	App	Tries	Goals	Pts
Wakefield Trinity	250	58	0	174
Leeds	165+2	93	0	279
Bradford Northern	63+4	18	0	54
Dewsbury	20	10	0	30
Yorkshire	2	1	0	3
England	3	1	0	3
Great Britain	5+1	0	0	0

Eric Harris

I must include Eric Harris in my list of heroes although I never saw him play. The reason for his inclusion is that I was brought up on the legend of the 'Toowoomba Ghost' by listening to stories of his exploits, for hours on end from Harris's biggest fan, my Dad. Since those protected days, sat with a cup of tea being enchanted by wonderful tales of pace and match-winning tries, I have had various coaching appointments that have allowed me to meet men who played in the same team as Eric Harris and they have given me an even deeper insight as to the brilliance of the man. It all started when the terrific Australian stand-off or centre, Jeff Moores took his first trip back home after signing at Headingley and returned in September 1930 with an unknown young Queenslander, Eric Harris, whom Moores had played alongside in Brisbane.

Tall and slim, Harris was of a quiet nature and it was his mentor, Moores, who looked after the studious man like a bodyguard. His first game for Leeds was against Featherstone Rovers at Headingley on 27 September and, although scoring a try, did not fill the demanding Leeds public with awe. But come Christmas Day, after only 17 matches, he had already passed the Leeds club record of 30 tries in a season established by Harold Buck in 1922-23. The legend was born.

To say he was fast is an understatement. Recorded comments by good players of the period testify to Eric's phenomenal pace and more specifically, his change of pace when he seemed to be already at his fastest. He would find another gear and accelerate "like a Rolls Royce", as one international full-back described.

In the 1932 Challenge Cup Final between Leeds and Swinton, with Leeds facing defeat, Harris was given a chance from well inside his own half. Striding clear of the cover, he was hemmed in on the touchline by that excellent defender Bob Scott, the Swinton full-back. Scott lined Harris up, went strongly into the tackle as he had done many times before when opposed by good wingmen, only to grab thin air. Harris had gone, long gone. It was a try to win the cup. Afterwards Scott was asked by local reporters how had Harris beaten him. "I don't know, he was there, then he wasn't, he was like a ghost," he replied. From that day, Harris was always nicknamed 'the Toowoomba Ghost'. Some six years later, again against Swinton again in the Championship semi-final at Headingley and behind 2-0, the unfortunate Swinton wingman McGurk dropped the ball and Harris scooped it up almost on his own 25 yard line. Setting his sails for the Swinton line, he outstripped all save the full-back Barnes, who must have been briefed by Scott about his change of pace. Harris headed infield, turned back towards the touchline and when Barnes shuffled to position himself for a touchline tackle, Harris simply glided back across the isolated defender to use his Olympic pace to scorch to the posts for the winner.

In the 1936 Challenge Cup Final at Wembley, Eric was involved in a controversial first try scored by Iowerth Isaac, after Harris had cross-kicked for the loose-forward to pick up and score. The Warrington players claimed offside but Stan Satterthwaite, who coached me as a youngster and played in that final, insisted that the cross-kick had been a planned move and that Isaac was well onside.

But again the try that won the cup for Leeds had no strings at all, it was a Harris special after he came inside from a Fred Harris pass, drifted passed three tacklers, chip-kicked ahead, re-gathered and burst between two more defenders to plant the ball over the line for a breathtaking try.

Eric Harris stayed at Leeds until his final game on 2 September 1939 against Bramley at Headingley when he scored his last try for the club.

He returned to Australia when war was declared, but left behind him a playing profile still talked about to this day. His outstanding club record of 391 tries in 383 games is extremely unlikely to be beaten and his joint club record, along with the old time Leeds forward, Fred Webster, of eight tries in a game. Webster's record was achieved against Coventry, Harris's against Bradford Northern, plus his 1935-36 record of 63 tries in a season will again take some breaking.

He played in a golden era with some superb centres beside him, such as Jeff Moores, Fred Harris, Stanley Brogden and Evan Williams, and with some excellent stand-offs to make room for him, Evan Williams, Dicky Ralph, Vic Hey and Oliver Morris. As I said, I never saw this hero, but I wish I had, even though I know every movement he made from my Dad's tales. Eric Harris is remembered by elderly gentlemen who recall warmer, sunnier days when the likes of Alf Ellerby, Brian Bevan, Lionel Cooper, Billy Batten, Mick Sullivan and Billy Boston roamed the touchline in search of tries.

	App	Tries	Goals	Pts
Leeds	383	391	16	1,205

Also played for Brisbane Wests and Toowoomba.

Dennis Hartley

A late starter in the game, Dennis went to the old Tattersfield ground, Doncaster and learned his trade very quickly indeed. A whopper of a lad, six-feet two-inches and 17 stones, it was obvious to all who saw him in his novice days that here was a class prop in the making. He was transferred to Hunslet in the early 1960s and settled down to form a renowned ball winning partnership with Bernard Prior, the former Leeds hooker, in the days of highly competitive scrums.

He was a 'yardage' man, one who would take the ball up all afternoon, and then some. Imagine the workload of the likes of 'Big D' in those days. First you had to work hard in the scrum, and I mean hard. You were pulling and pushing a guy, never any lighter than, say 16 stones, and looking after your hooker to boot. You were doing your share of the round the play-the-ball tackling then driving the ball away from your own half and being expected to support near your opponents line or even run off a set move to use your strength and score. Oh yes, there was never a dull moment.

Gradually the selectors began to notice the big lad and in 1964 he was selected to represent Great Britain in the two test matches against France. The season after Dennis realised another dream when Hunslet's excellent Challenge Cup run saw them beat Wakefield Trinity in the semi-final and march on to Wembley to play the strong Wigan side. This 1965 final has gone down in history as the best under the old unlimited tackle rule, with Wigan winning a nail-biter 20-16.

Not long after that match, Dennis moved on again to Castleford who became one of the strongest clubs around in the late 1960s and early 1970s. The pairing of Dennis and Johnny Ward, then Dennis and Clive Dickinson, ensured plenty of ball from the scrum for the exciting Castleford half-backs, Keith Hepworth and Alan Hardisty, and the awesome power and football skills of a young Malcolm Reilly. Again Dennis was rewarded for his great efforts by being selected for Great Britain against the French in 1968 and 1969, the latter being a good year as Castleford went to Wembley to beat Salford 11-6 and give Dennis his Challenge Cup winners medal.

If 1969 was a good year then 1970 was even better, as off to Wembley Dennis and his Castleford team-mates went again, this time to beat a good Wigan side 7-2 in a match remembered for a tackle that put the Wigan full-back out of the game and into dreamland. Two winners medals in two years made those hard seasons of learning the game at lowly Doncaster all worthwhile, and there was more to come as 'Big D' was selected for the 1970 Lions tour of Australia and New Zealand, and what a squad it was. The Great Britain front-row of Dennis Hartley, Tony Fisher and Cliff Watson put the frighteners on the Aussie pack and even the old Australian warrior, Arthur Beetson, could do nothing with them. Behind them a second-row of Doug Laughton and Jimmy Thompson was hard enough to play against but then there was Mal Reilly at loose-forward. Goodness me, what a pack! This 1970 touring side must rank as the best ever and Dennis held his own in it.

The highlight of his tour must have been the try he scored in the final test. John Atkinson with two, Syd Hynes and Roger Millward scored tries but there was a beauty from Dennis who charged 30 yards to dive over and bring the house down. On this tour Great Britain played, in all, 24 games, 17 in Australia and seven in New Zealand. They won 22, lost one and drew one - a fabulous record.

Dennis played in many finals, the Championship Final against Leeds at Odsal in 1969, a couple of Yorkshire Cup Finals and two BBC Floodlit Trophy wins: 7-2 against Swinton in 1967, and 8-5 against Leigh in 1968.

Dennis, although starting late, made up for that in spades. The likeable giant put a lot back into the game when he finally retired and he went into coaching on the Castleford staff. His work with the youngsters, showing the ropes, teaching them skills and giving sound football advice, went a long way in producing that endless conveyor belt of good professional players regularly seen at Castleford.

But I remember Dennis in the early 1960s as a big, strong, willing lad who dropped the ball a bit, thank goodness, because he was not the type of bloke that you wanted to tackle regularly. I managed a few games against him just before I retired and recall that it was always ankle deep in mud when we played at Doncaster. Later Dennis and I were on the RFL's coaching scheme course at Lilleshall together - the big lad was always great company and it is not hard to understand why he had a successful junior coaching spell after playing. The kids adored him. To any youngster looking to do well in our game I would advise them to look up 'Big D' and talk to him.

	App	Tries	Goals	Pts
Doncaster	116	8	11	46
Hunslet	200	23	1	71
Castleford	259+9	15	2	49
Yorkshire	9	0	0	0
Great Britain	11	1	0	3

John Holmes

John signed for Leeds as a youngster and made his first team debut as a teenage full-back in 1968. He was introduced to the club by the former Leeds and Castleford forward, Alan Horsfall, who was coaching Kirkstall Boys Club at the time. John was a tall, gangling youth and possessed all the natural skills that earmarked him as a future international, but the problem for Leeds was that while young John was obviously a good player, where would they play him? His six feet one inch frame had not filled out enough and he still had teenage strength rather than the mature strength required for either the centre or stand-off positions that the club hoped he would fill in later years. So at first he was played at full-back.

At that time, in the late 1960s and early 1970s, John was also a prolific goalkicker and on his debut, against Hunslet in the Lazenby Cup, landed a hatful of goals to mark him as the next long term points scorer in a traditional line of kickers in the club's history. In his first full season, 1970-71, assisted by some terrific try scorers - Bob Haigh, John Atkinson, Alan Smith and Syd Hynes to mention just four - John Holmes kicked a phenomenal 159 goals and finished third in the kickers' list behind Kel Coslett and Stuart Ferguson, but in front of a string of world class goalkickers, David Watkins, Colin Tyrer, Neil Fox and Terry Clawson.

Strangely, although he kicked goals for Great Britain, John never figured again in the top goalkickers at club level. I once asked him what happened and he said: "I just didn't want that mind-bending responsibility that goes with goalkicking. I didn't mind it now and again but not all the time on top of the responsibilities of being a playmaker". I can understand those feelings because not every player, even the good goalkickers, likes that overpowering pressure.

John's versatility can be seen when checking the positions he played in when the various big games came around. He was at full-back in 1970-71 in most of the club's games, yet was selected at left centre on his Great Britain debut the same year. In 1972 he played at right centre for the national team and stand-off in several club games. So it continued: full-back, centre and stand-off for Leeds, centre for Great Britain, until the selection for his biggest games yet: the World Cup series held in France in 1972. Playing for the first time at stand-off for his country, John starred in the win over New Zealand in Pau and kicked 10 goals and scored two tries in the 53-19 demolition of the Kiwis. Seven days later, on 11 November, John was at stand-off again in the 10-10 draw against Australia at Lyon that gave Great Britain the title of World Champions.

His record 26 points (in those days a try was worth three points) against New Zealand was the most scored by a Great Britain player in any type of international and was only beaten when Bobbie Goulding scored 32 against Fiji in 1996. The 1970s was a productive time in John Holmes's career, gaining 19 of his 20 Great Britain caps in that era, the final one was gained in the disastrous test series against Australia in 1982.

Success also followed in club football. John appeared in four Wembley finals in the 1970s, losing to Leigh in 1971 and Saints in 1972, but picking up two winners medals in wins over Widnes in 1977 and Saints in 1978. Three Regal Trophy finals gave John one runners up medal in 1983 against Wigan and two winners - in 1973 against Salford and in 1984 against Widnes, when I was lucky enough to coach Leeds. He was at full-back when Leeds beat Saints in the 1975 Premiership Final at Wigan and played in seven Yorkshire Cup-winning sides from 1971 to 1981.

His eight Yorkshire caps are supplemented by seven England caps earned between 1975 and 1978. This superb record is remarkable because of the number of positions John played regularly for his club, county and country. In the early 1980s John played a couple of games for Leeds in the second-row and at loose-forward but, for a player who achieved a rare honour by being granted two testimonial seasons by the Rugby Football League, the pack was not for him and after sustaining a broken jaw late in his career, he coached a bit with the 'A' team at Leeds.

I remember him consoling me after being beaten in the 1984 Challenge Cup semi-final by Widnes. A player consoling the coach is very unusual indeed, but he did it in his nice, gentle way, a true gentleman. John suffered a very close, personal loss a few years ago when his dear wife died, but the brilliant former footballer still has a wry smile when we meet. I used to tell him that the reason why he and his elder brother Phil, who also played at Leeds but moved across to Batley to serve many seasons at Mount Pleasant, were such good players was because of their parents' fish and chip shop in the Beechwoods, just below the Headingley ground. The fish was beautiful. Just right for a Headingley hero.

	App	Tries	Goals	Pts
Leeds	608+18	153	553	1,554
Yorkshire	8	1	8	19
Great Britain	14+6	3	22	51
England	5+2	5	0	15

Dick Huddart

We in rugby league tend to categorize players into niches. Big, tough, beefy men are usually front-rowers; small, quick, wiry men are usually half-backs and tall, athletic, fast-running men are normally considered wingmen, centres or back-row forwards. If any of those players was lucky enough to have the gift of pace, power, strength, running skills and toughness in defence added to their physical attributes then he would be called Dick Huddart.

Even his youthful background was rugged. Born in the wilds of Cumberland, Dick possessed a natural hardness gained from the generations of Cumberland men who toiled in the coal mines that burrowed out under the treacherous Irish Sea. The area in which Dick was born and grew up was, in those days, an outpost, a series of small towns clung with finger tips to the hills and mountainsides of the county that even the Roman Legions found too difficult to overpower.

Dick signed with his local club, Whitehaven, with its tradition of always providing the best teams with hard opposition to beat. Not a fashionable, big city club, but one full of local players, although many moved to greener pastures. It was said in those days that all the good clubs had one or two Cumbrians in their sides, and the team that Dick joined was a group of big, young, strong lads who would die for the Cumberland cause, plus they were hungry for the glitter of success and all that went with the good money and notoriety.

Dick's first real chance of the big time came on a murky, April afternoon in 1957, when the home-spun Whitehaven took on the 'Bank of England' side, Leeds, at Odsal in the semi-final of the Challenge Cup. The other semi-final that year was between Leigh and star-studded Barrow. This gave the Whitehaven boys added incentive because, should Barrow beat the redoubtable cup fighters from Leigh, and Whitehaven could beat Leeds, it would set up a terrific north west coast final at Wembley. In ankle deep mud, as was often the case at Odsal, Whitehaven's pack, which included Dick, blasted Leeds apart with their tenacity and sheer will-to-win. As the time ebbed away, the Cumberland boys were in front 9-8. Twice in that pulsating second half, with Wembley beckoning, the Whitehaven pack carried the ball the full length of the field with simple picking-up and running from the dummy-half position. Every man was a hero as the seconds ticked away and news came over the tannoy that Leigh and Barrow had drawn, 2-2, at Wigan. But suddenly, in injury time, the Leeds international scrum-half, Jeff Stevenson grabbed the ball and struck a superb drop-goal, worth two points then, to win this most exciting cup tie 10-9.

The disappointment was only eased later when Dick was selected to tour with the 1958 Lions and cemented his place in the Great Britain side on that tour, scoring 17 tries in a mammoth 24 appearances out of a possible 30. Dick joined St Helens on his return from tour, on 15 October 1958. This move helped turn the former Whitehaven second rower into a legend. When he finally played at Wembley, Dick starred in Saints 12-6 win over Wigan in 1961 and won the coveted Lance Todd Trophy for the best player in the final. He also figured in several Lancashire Cup successes as Saints dominated that competition in the early 1960s. Dick toured again in 1962 and again appeared in an amazing 23 games out of the 30 played in Australia and New Zealand, scoring the most tries for a forward on that tour with 13. In all, Dick played in 16 international matches for Great Britain, the last one in 1963 and shortly after accepted an offer to join the St George club in Sydney.

He played in, and scored a try in, the 1966 Grand Final win for St George over Balmain and became one of the elite players who hold Challenge Cup and Australian Grand Final winners medals. A tremendous forward who was dangerous when running with the ball both in Britain or Australia, Dick combined power and extreme pace with clever skills. One of the original 'wide running' forwards, Dick was used intelligently by most of his coaches as his power against centres and half-backs was almost unstoppable. A fearsome sight when try-bound, this big, strong man, standing six-feet three-inches and weighing in at around 16 stone, possessed a hard hand-off and a subtle swerve when at full gallop.

His epitaph should be: 'Spectators and supporters of all teams would pay money to watch him in action'. He is still revered in this country more than 40 years after his last game here and his abilities are not only remembered in Whitehaven and St Helens but throughout the rugby league world in general.

To have seen Dick Huddart play was a pleasure, to have played against him on two occasions was an honour and to write about him, a privilege. A super hero, Dick Huddart, Great Britain.

	App	Tries	Goals	Pts
Whitehaven	72	12	0	36
St Helens	209	76	0	228
St George (Sydney)	78+1	16	0	48
Cumberland	11	4	0	12
Great Britain	16	2	0	6
England	1	0	0	0

Dai Jenkins

A muddy ground, steam rising from two sets of forwards striving to win the ball, a small figure suddenly emerging from the gloom around the blind side of the pack, a perfectly judged grubber kick, end-over-end, rolling over the touchline some 20 yards up-field. Then a scrum some 10 yards from the opponents' try line, a quick heel, the scrum-half shoots away, taking his opposite number and loose-forward with him, a deft back-flipped pass and Ike Owens the Leeds loose-forward went in for another try.

Those are just two of the many wonderful skills that I can see now, in my mind's eye, produced by the fabulous Dai Jenkins or 'Jenks' - master footballer, master tactician, and master scrum-half. Dai lived in the Ashvilles, a row of streets with the railway cutting at one end and Cardigan Road - which led to the holy of holies, Headingley Football and Cricket Ground - at the other, after he had spent some time as the landlord of the Town Hall Tavern, a public house that was tenanted by a series of Leeds rugby league players.

As kids going to school up Cardigan Road, we used to see Dai now and again, and would always get a little wave or a wink of his eye if we called over to him. He was the old-fashioned type of half-back, brilliant hands, great short kicking game, good copy book close in tackler. He was always around his pack of forwards, never straying far from them, snapping at their heels and urging them onward, onward, forever onward. Scrum-halves were mostly the same then, Tommy Bradshaw, Herbert Goodfellow, Tommy McCue and many more, small men with hearts like lions, skilful footballers, many maintaining the innate skills of the rugby union half-backs whose main armoury was the kicking game. But these rugby league men also ran with the ball.

If not the whole-hearted sprinters of later years, these men would fetch and carry for the forwards, they would drive the pack like a drover's dog drives the cattle and sheep in Australia, or the sheepdog manoeuvres a flock into a pen on the Cumbrian fells, then, when in the correct area, they would dart for the line, or a gap in the opposition defence, usually with a shadow, their team's loose-forward right on their tails.

Another Welshman, Ike Owens, was Dai's regular loose-forward. Alf Watson played if Ike was out for some reason. Owens was a speedster, lightening-fast and a great cover tackler, but Dai's best mate was the grand old hooker, Con Murphy, yet another Welshman who had gone to the fledgling London club, Acton & Willesden with Dai from Wales. They

69

both joined Streatham & Mitcham when the west London side withdrew from the Rugby Football League after one season.

Both Con and Dai then joined the Leeds club at Christmas 1936. Dai managed only one Great Britain cap, in the home series against New Zealand in 1947, but did make the tour to Australia and New Zealand in 1946. He played in 11 games on tour, but the outstanding form of the experienced Tommy McCue meant that Dai played in the bush and up-country matches.

An ever-popular player at Headingley, Dai was at the heart of the great Leeds team of the late 1940s and particularly the 1946-47 side that reached Wembley without a point being scored against them. The cup run had started on 8 March 1947 with a 12-0 win, in the first leg of the two-legged first round tie as they did then, against Barrow at home. The blizzard conditions of that winter meant the second leg was played at Headingley again and Dai Jenkins scored a good try in Leeds's 6-0 win. Hunslet fell, 5-0, in round two and with Jenkins at his best against Tommy Bradshaw, round three brought a tremendous 5-0 win at Central Park, Wigan. The semi-final saw another great show by Jenkins as Leeds stormed to Wembley on the back of a resounding 21-0 win over Wakefield Trinity at Huddersfield's Fartown ground.

Tales of fall-outs in the Leeds dressing room and threats of strikes before the Wembley final did the team and Dai Jenkins no good at all. Rumour had it that Ike Owens and Dai had argued and that the team had refused to accept the level of pay promised to them if they won. Wanting more than the directors would pay, the team was given an ultimatum by club chairman, Sir Edwin Airey: "play for our offer or the 'A' team can play". The team turned up but were outplayed and outsmarted by a very experienced Bradford Northern side who won the cup 8-4. In 1948-49 Dai Jenkins ended his stint with Leeds and, as most players did in those days, moved to a smaller club, Bramley. The heady days of touring and Wembley appearances behind him, Dai played a while at Barley Mow, then at Keighley before leaving the sport he loved and had graced. The classical, tough, skilful, thinking footballer was a role model for kids in the North Leeds district; in fact, a hero.

	App	Tries	Goals	Pts
Acton & Willesden	33	3	0	9
Streatham & Mitcham	20	5	0	15
Leeds	292	55	7	179
Bramley	25	1	0	3
Keighley	65	5	2	19
Great Britain	1	1	0	3
Wales	17	1	0	3

Lewis Jones

I was present when B. L. Jones trotted onto 'God's green acre', Headingley, for his first ever game for Leeds. He was Lewis Jones, the golden boy of Welsh rugby, Jones of Llanelli and Wales, the wonder boy, Jones the scourge of the Five Nations, Jones the 'boot'. He was all those things and even more.

I can see him now: thinning golden hair, the slightly bowed legs of a true footballer, the athletic build, not massive like the superb Neil Fox, but, as my Dad, who was a good judge of a player, said: "Big enough". His signing, for £6,000, had set the North of England alight with the thought of being able to see in the flesh this tremendous points scorer from the valleys. Rugby union as a whole was shattered to think that its shining star had defected and 'gone North', the Welsh could no longer boast that Lewis Jones was wearing the scarlet jersey and the huge crowds at Llanelli would no longer rise as one to glory in 'the golden boy'.

He now wore the blue and amber of the proud Leeds Rugby League Club, and very soon the thousands of excited spectators who crammed into the palatial home of that club would see just what the Welsh were so boastful of. The crowd obviously wanted to see what this £6,000 man could do in his first match at full-back against Keighley, remembering that in the early 1950s, £6,000 was a prince's ransom.

Taking a pass from a scrum, Jones sliced between the two Keighley centres, yet looked to have no chance as they closed down on the Welsh wizard, but with a long stride and a kick of those bowed legs, he showed, for the first time, that magnificent change of pace that became his trademark for so many years and he shot into the clear to give a walk-in try to the supporting Leeds player. Not since the legendary Australian wingman, Eric Harris in the early 1930s had the Leeds public seen that tremendous evasive quality, and how they relished it.

Lewis Jones became a household name in the West Riding of Yorkshire from that moment and people came to look in wonder at the skills this 'Prince of Wales' displayed, week after week. The man was sensational in everything he did in rugby football.

He was a revelation with his goalkicking style too. No matter what the distance, he took only three paces back and, in the old-fashioned toe-ended way, strode to the ball and whacked the ball into the wide, blue yonder. In rugby league goalkickers usually took a good run, to gain maximum power through momentum. Jones dispelled the theory that this was necessary in a few moments of his first game, as the crowd held its breath and Jones took the first of hundreds of successful kicks at goal at Headingley. His run was based on pure timing and rhythm, never seen before in rugby league.

A serious broken arm at Batley from a perfectly fair tackle by John Etty, the great Batley wingman, almost ended a glorious career before it started, but Jones came back to gain 15 Great Britain caps and tour with the Dickie Williams led side in 1954. On that tour Lewis kicked 127 goals and scored 8 tries for a total of 278 points. This tour is remembered for a game against New South Wales in which all the players were sent off for fighting and the match abandoned, but Lewis never committed a dirty act in his life. The thin golden hair disappeared completely as the years progressed and Lewis Jones, like wine, bettered with age.

Some people said he was not a good tackler. Possibly because, like all class players, he was not forced to run around like a wild man, the game came naturally to this laid-back maestro, but believe me he was a strong tackler, as I found out playing against him on several occasions. His passing of the ball was excellent and when Jones played at stand-off with the former Welsh rugby union scrum-half, Colin Evans as his partner at Leeds, they worked a run-around move together in which Jones hung out a pass behind him for Evans to run onto. It was incredible to see as the ball appeared to float in the air.

When I was asked to apply for the Dewsbury coaching job and turned up to be interviewed, the second man also being seen was my hero, Lewis Jones, who had left Leeds after many seasons to take up a coaching job at the wealthy junior club of Wentworthville, on the outskirts of Sydney, and had done well with them. I was overawed that I should be considered on the same planet as Lewis Jones, but, luckily, I got the job and he was superb about it, the perfect gentleman, and a real hero.

	App	Tries	Goals	Pts
Leeds	385	144	1,244	2,920
Wales	1	0	5	10
Great Britain	15	5	66	147

Vince Karalius

The great Vince Karalius toured as a Lion only once, in 1958, but did enough to be dubbed by the Australian press, the 'Wild Bull of the Pampas'. So tough and uncompromising was the St Helens legendary loose-forward that he seemed to terrorise the Australian pack all on his own. Considering the company he had to play alongside on that particular tour, including Brian McTigue, Eric Prescott, Ken Jackson, Brian Edgar, Dick Huddart, John Whiteley, Alvin Ackerley, Dennis Goodwin, Mick Martin, Tommy Harris and Abe Terry, that was some accolade to be given.

The fact that Vince toured only that once must make the reader realise that there was a wealth of terrific back-rowers available to the selectors at that time - Dave Valentine, Ken Traill, John Whiteley, Roy Evans, Derek Turner and Harry Street all were loose-forwards. If you added a list of second-rowers who could all play at number 13 it would fill this book, that was the strength of our game at the time.

When Vince signed as a youngster for Saints, he was a fitness fanatic and because of this never carried any excess bodyweight. He was, therefore, a little light, but his toughness usually saw him through. Vince was also in the habit, so the legend goes, of running to his home in Widnes after training at St Helens, to boost his stamina. The bodyweight problem was solved when Vince went into the army to do his national service. Having more time to concentrate on a savage weight training programme, Vince came back to Saints, not only heavier in bodyweight, but unbelievably stronger.

He was now the perfect size to mix it with the few players who gave him a hard time before national service built him up, notably one clash with the renowned Harry Bath, the great Australian who played for Warrington. In one of Vince's last games before joining the army, Harry had, because of his bigger size, given him a rough time, but acceptable retribution was taken on Vince's return when he completely outplayed the famous Aussie.

Vince won 12 Great Britain caps, 10 while at Saints and two when he transferred to his home town club of Widnes. Vince also led a cracking Widnes side to Wembley where they beat Hull Kingston Rovers in the 1964 Challenge Cup Final. Vince's cousin, the great Frank Myler, played in the centre and was a try-scorer in that game.

After finishing his illustrious playing career, Vince went into coaching and was successful twice with Widnes on the Wembley trail: his charges beating Warrington 14-7 in 1975, then in 1984 his Widnes team beat

Wigan 19-6. In between he had a three-year stint at Wigan as coach from 1976 to 1979.

As a leader and wholehearted player Vince had few betters. In an era of great loose-forwards he was never out of the top two. His defence bordered on the fanatical and on a few occasions I had experience of that. In one game at Knowsley Road we were bringing the ball out of our own '25' and having kept my eye on the ball to receive it, I then glanced up to find a gap to run into, but what I saw was Vince Karalius, airborne and coming straight at me, his legs spread in front of him like a giant pair of shears. Hitting simultaneously with those big legs and strong arms, he wrapped me up, as he had wrapped up hundreds before me, at the same time twisting me around so that he finished on top of the tackle with a thud.

Later in the season he caught me again with that crunching tackle, with exactly the same technique, and the same end product. It was a vice-like, shuddering experience and, no doubt, if it had been a test match I wouldn't have got up, even on shaking legs.

His ability to pass the ball accurately with tacklers all around him was a gift too and when one looks back on the clashes between Vince and any one of the five or six top-line loose-forwards of the day, you begin to realise just how tough and skilful they were. I coached Vince's nephew, 'young' Tony, at Wigan and he told me of the accident, in the family's scrap iron business yard that robbed Vince of two of his fingers. Lifting a huge girder with one of his brothers, the girder slipped and when his brother came over to check all was OK, Vince had just picked something off the floor. Turning to his sibling, he said, as cool as you like, "Just run me to the hospital will you and I'll see if they can stitch these back on". In his other hand he held his severed fingers! More than just a hero: a tough hero.

	App	Tries	Goals	Pts
St Helens	252	41	0	123
Widnes	132	6	0	18
Lancashire	10	1	0	3
Great Britain	12	0	0	0

Arthur Keegan

I remember an article that appeared in *League Weekly*, in which a very good former player selected a side of successful players, all of whom had come from the Dewsbury and Batley districts, also known as the Heavy Woollen area. Arthur Keegan was selected at full-back in that team, ahead of several excellent last-line defenders, and was well worthy of the place. I remember watching a young Keegan play in a curtain-raiser before a Dewsbury versus Salford game at Crown Flatt and thinking: "This kid looks a good prospect" because he stood out with a fine array of skills. Little did I know that 17 years later I would be working with him as his assistant coach at the Bramley club. But it was in 1957 that this stocky, hard-tackling full-back took my eye, as he also took the eye of the Hull FC directors who signed him as a professional in 1958. His junior rugby had been learned in the hard school of the Yorkshire under-15s and under-17s and his club was from the area in which he lived, West Town Boys, Dewsbury, in the Catholic parish of St Polonius.

The major senior amateur club in the district was the famous Dewsbury Celtic, for whom Arthur's elder brother James was a regular player, and any player not signed as a professional nearly always signed to play for the Celtic. This very successful club was run from the Irish National Club and was within the West Town district which indeed held a large number of Anglo-Irish Catholic families. However, at the time Arthur signed for Hull, West Town Boys were not under the Dewsbury Celtic umbrella and were an independent club.

Almost immediately after signing for Hull, Arthur was installed in the first team and fulfilled a childhood ambition by playing in a side that won its way to Wembley in his first season. The end result though was a 30-13 defeat at the hands of the excellent Wigan outfit in the 1959 Final before a crowd of 79,811 spectators. A couple of Yorkshire Cup Finals came his way and selection for the Yorkshire county team, for whom he played in successive teams from beating the touring Kiwis 15-8 on 20 September 1965 at Castleford, through to 1 October, 1969, when Yorkshire beat Cumberland 42-3 at Hull Kingston Rovers' Craven Park.

His crowning glory though was when he was chosen to tour with the 1966 Lions in Australia and New Zealand. Two full-backs were selected, Arthur and Ken Gowers of Swinton, Arthur looked like being second choice when Gowers was named vice-captain of the tour, but his good form in the matches before the first test earned him the crucial number one jersey in the opening test at the Sydney Cricket Ground. A fantastic 17-13 win for Great Britain saw Arthur kick three vital goals.

The second test played in Brisbane was a titanic struggle with Arthur kicking two penalty goals against three from Ken Barnes for Australia which won the game for the home side 6-4. The closeness of the score is put into perspective when one realises that Great Britain had Bill Ramsey sent off early in the game.

Arthur Keegan won nine full international caps, two in 1966 on tour, two against France at Carcassonne and Wigan in 1967, three against the touring Australians again in 1967 at Leeds, London's White City and Swinton, one against France in 1968 at St Helens and the final one against France in 1969 at Toulouse.

Arthur stayed loyal to the Hull club until 1972 when he moved to Bramley to become assistant to the former Wakefield Trinity star, Keith Holliday. As player-coach after Holliday's departure, Arthur moulded the Bramley side into a hard team to beat, particularly on their home ground of McLaren Field, but a bigger success was just around the corner. Bramley had never won a major trophy in their history but under Arthur's superb leadership and rock like defence they won the BBC2 Floodlight Trophy in the 1972-73 season. Two wonderful wins were achieved in this fine cup run; St Helens fell at Bramley and the final win against the cup kings Widnes, at Naughton Park brought the trophy home to Bramley.

Arthur's fine playing career ended after he moved to Batley when he suffered a badly broken jaw, ironically against Bramley.

He was always a gentleman who put those who spoke to him at ease. But to see him manoeuvre an opponent to the touchline, then scythe him down with a perfect leg tackle into touch is my memory of one of the most respected of our game's heroes, 'The rock of the Boulevard'.

	App	Tries	Goals	Pts
Hull FC	365+1	31	318	729
Bramley	130+5	21	71	205
Batley	6	0	0	0
Yorkshire	13	3	7	23
Great Britain	9	1	5	13
England	2	0	0	0

Brett Kenny

It would be totally unfair to include Peter Sterling in this collection and leave out Brett Kenny. It would be like fish without chips, or bread without butter. Kenny and Sterling were synonymous. From being youngsters they trained together, played football together - not only as team-mates, but as stand-off and scrum-half, blood brothers, soul mates, best pals. They toured twice together and they were written in the record books together. They won test matches together, won grand finals together and they were inseparable.

The Brett Kenny I first saw was a tall, skinny kid, playing one game at stand-off and the next game in the centre. Young-looking and very laid-back with his relaxed attitude, he burst into action when in possession of the ball or when called on to defend. His pace was electric, he was very sharp off the mark and with the ability to accelerate while appearing to be already running flat out. Brett caught out many experienced defenders with this ploy. His swerve while travelling at a high rate of knots was allied to a tremendous hand-off, like the kick of a mule, and he possessed a neat sidestep, off either foot, that made him just about the best attacking runner of his era.

Like most star Australian players, his background from when he was a child had taught him that rugby league was a team game, he knew not to be greedy when having made a clean break, but to make sure it was finished off with a try, but it mattered not who scored the try. Therefore Kenny made many, many tries for his team-mates, as did his partner, Sterling. Some theorists thought that this was the Australian secret of success, machine-like in their approach, and totally in control through perfect skill and pace co-ordination. Well maybe so, but I think it was simpler than that. I think it was just that players such as Sterling, Kenny and Wally Lewis were simply brilliant, natural footballers, who knew, through instinct, when to pass and when to dummy, when to move into the tackle and how to tackle. Kenny was possibly quicker than both Sterling and Lewis, the best actual rugby player of the three.

On the 1982 tour, Wally Lewis was the first choice stand-off and Kenny a utility middle back one who could play anywhere from full-back to stand-off. Lewis was the vice captain behind the skipper, hooker Max Krilich of Manly-Warringah. But the crafty 'cranky' Australian coach Frankie Stanton, saw the playing power of Kenny and compared the 'game-maker' Lewis to the 'game-breaker' Kenny. Stanton went for Brett as first choice stand-off in all three tests. It caused consternation among the Queenslanders in the squad, because to them Wally was king, an icon in north eastern Australia, and a big personal friend of Senator Ron McAuliffe, the political leader of Queensland, a once potential Prime Minister of Australia and still a very, very powerful man.

But Stanton dug his heels in, withstood the political tornado, and came out the other side with an unbeaten record, the first Australian coach and team to do it.

Brett came over here to play for the great Wigan club and guided them to a terrific win at Wembley in 1985 when, along with fellow Australian, John Ferguson who scored two tries in the victory, the Lancastrians defeated a very good Hull FC who had Peter Sterling at scrum-half. Brett also registered a superb try in that final.

Kenny played 17 times in Australia's green and gold jersey and the same number of matches in the blue of New South Wales. In club rugby, again like Sterling, Parramatta Eels were his only Australian club. He was very successful during his time at the Parramatta Stadium. Whether playing in the centre, or at stand-off half, Brett Kenny was a world-class player.

His regular partner in test and club football, when at stand-off, was Peter Sterling or very occasionally Steve Mortimer. His partners when operating at centre always scored a glut of tries, as the records of such as Michael O'Connor, Kerry Boustead, Eric Grothe, Chris Anderson, Les Kiss and Dale Shearer show.

As he matured, the slim figure turned into a good-sized middle-back and because he was tall the extra few pounds were easily carried. His effortless stride devoured the ground and that shimmering swerve and exaggerated body lean as he as he rounded an opponent, I can still see today. A superb athlete, Brett Kenny could have made it at almost any sport because his athleticism was allied to a passion for winning.

He was a winner, and the number of games, mostly at club level, that Brett won for his team in the dying minutes of the match are legend. I witnessed one such try at the Sydney Cricket Ground, one Friday evening in July 1985 against Souths for the Eels, scored by Brett in the last seconds after a 70-yard run. A winning try scored by a hero.

	App	Tries	Goals	Pts
Parramatta	264	110	0	410
Wigan	25	19	0	76
New South Wales	16+1	2	0	8
Australia	17	10	0	36

Terry Langton

In the 1970s, if asked "Who is the toughest scrum half around?", many players would answer Reg Bowden or Paul Woods, but sometimes the name of Terry Langton would crop up and the reaction would be: "Oh yes, I forgot about him, he was a tough 'un". I was coaching the amateur club Stanningley around 1970 and was desperately short of good players. We had gained the services of a Bramley rugby union player, 'Budge' Lynn, who was enjoying the atmosphere in rugby league when there was a 'dust up' in the clubhouse at the union club and six players were banned for fighting. 'Budge' was a big mate of these players and he asked them to change codes and come to their local amateur rugby league club with him. As coach I remembered the tale from Headingley, told since I was a kid, about the Leeds club refusing to give Brian Bevan a trial, and dismissing him out of hand, because he didn't look the part. One of my first lessons as a coach came directly from that story - always have a look at anyone who wants to join you because he could be another Brian Bevan. Of the six who came from the union club, four went on to play regular first team professional rugby league and the other two could have, but preferred to stay in the amateur game.

Terry Langton was one of the future professionals. His brother Barry was as good as him, and when paired together, with Terry at scrum-half and Barry at stand-off, they were excellent - tough, durable, never say die, sensible good footballers and winners. A younger Langton came later when Stephen signed for Hunslet and played for many seasons when the older siblings had retired.

Terry was the only scrum-half I ever saw who had a cauliflower ear; he was always in the thick of the action. The former international forward and after-dinner speaker, Mick Morgan, who played with Terry at Wakefield, said that in his opinion, "Terry could start an argument in an empty house and would sooner have a fight than have his dinner". But his value to any team was inestimable. He never lost a 50-50 ball. He very rarely missed a tackle, either on a back or a forward. The word was he preferred knocking forwards over, and his strong bursts from the base of the scrum brought him many tries from scrums close to the line.

I was rebuilding at Halifax and wanted Terry with me at Thrum Hall. Ron Dobson and I talked the board into making a bid to the Wakefield directors for him as I had found out Terry wanted to leave Belle Vue. A deal was struck: £750 for the best young scrum-half in the county, and to be paid in instalments. The deal was £250 down and £250 at the start of the next two seasons.

Like almost all rugby league players in those days, Terry liked a pint. It was a hilarious experience to be out on the town with Terry and Barry, but after a few drinks they were more like Rocky Marciano and Sonny Liston, when they drank together.

Their brother-in-law, Keith Waites, a cracking wingman, joined us at Halifax from Bramley and he too was a card, adept at winding up Terry and they were the life and soul of our team bus, on those long trips home on the M62. Terry would sing his heart out, forgetting the words, and Keith would whisper asides to keep him singing.

Out one Christmas Eve after work, Terry arrived for early evening training and at first Keith managed to keep him out of my sight. But I noticed something was wrong when Terry appeared ready to go out for a light session on the field and had both his legs in one leg hole of his shorts, yet hadn't noticed. I let him off and he had a blinder in the Boxing Day game at Thrum Hall.

Going into the trenches, you needed Terry Langton with you. He would never give you anything less than 100 per cent effort and was a cheeky little devil. Short in height, but very strong and sturdily built, he didn't get his ear by standing back. In fact ultra-tough forwards like Terry Dewhirst, Peter Jarvis, Alan Wood and Tony Garforth, used to shout at him, when the serious tackling was taking place, "What are you doing in here you little -------, get out of it, we want you running, not tackling", but they couldn't get rid of him as easy as that.

On a Blackpool end-of-season trip, Terry was thrown bodily into the deep water under the Log Flume on the Pleasure Beach because he was cheeky to the forwards and, as he surfaced he called "Help, can't swim" and went under. Mick Scott was in mid-swallow dive, fully clothed, to save him when he came up again, laughed and called: "Fooled you", and struck out like Mark Spitz for the bank, with Scotty in mid-air, shouting "You little ------", before he hit the water.

Terry went back into amateur rugby league and now serves the West Bowling Club in Bradford as chairman. Always at his best when circumstances required his best, he had what it takes and was a big-hearted, highly popular hero.

	App	Tries	Goals	Pts
Wakefield Trinity	30+15	5	0	15
Halifax	184+5	44	4	143
Mansfield	57+9	15	0	60

Great Britain versus New Zealand 1985

Top: Ian Potter, Ellery Hanley, Shaun Edwards & Maurice Bamford after the third test at Elland Road.

Middle: Maurice Bamford & David Watkinson after the third test.

Bottom: Des Drummond makes a break in the second test at Wigan.

(Photos: Andrew Cudbertson)

Leeds' Bell making a break for Leeds against Widnes in the
Challenge Cup semi-final 1984 (Photo: Andrew Cudbertson)

Andy Farrell charging forward (Photo: RLphotos.com)

Alex Murphy on the attack (Photo: Courtesy Alex Service)

Cliff Watson scoring for St Helens (Photo: Courtesy Alex Service)

Dick Huddart fends off an opponent
(Photo: Courtesy Alex Service)

Tom van Vollenhoven makes a break in the snow
(Photo: Courtesy Alex Service)

Mick Sullivan – a Great Britain hero.
(Photo: Courtesy Alex Service)

Wally Lewis

They say that only the great players are hated by their opponents' supporters, well Wally Lewis was an enigma, hated by every New South Welshman when he played for Queensland, yet loved by them when wearing the green and gold of Australia.

Despite many offers, Wally Lewis would not leave his native Brisbane to play in the big city, Sydney. His detractors in the south said it was because he could not handle the hard, week-in, week-out, no-nonsense Sydney football and that he knew he would be found out by its intensity. But suggest that to a Queenslander and the reply would be unprintable. They would point out that Lewis was in all the record-breaking Australian international sides of recent years and was an integral member of both the 'Invincibles' of 1982 and the 'Unbeatables' of 1986, the pair of touring sides that went through a European tour with an unblemished record.

Wally, whose nickname of 'Gator' stemmed from the American television cartoon character Wally Gator, was a top class rugby union schoolboy player as well as enjoying success in the 13-a-side code and his wish, on both codes' account, was for Queensland to be the top dog in everything. Wally's biggest admirer was Senator Ron McAuliffe, one of Queensland's representatives in the Australian Senate who, it was thought, funded the movement that managed to keep Wally playing his rugby in north east Australia.

Lewis, always the golden boy in his home state, found difficulty adjusting to the attitudes of New South Wales coaches and his clashes with 'cranky' Frank Stanton, the coach of the 1982 tour, when Lewis was vice-captain, are well documented. So anti-Lewis and Queensland did Stanton become, that Wally was left out of the starting team for the first two tests, his place going to the excellent Brett Kenny. Terry Fearnley followed Stanton as Australia's coach and again there was no love lost between coach and player.

Wally had a spell playing in Britain in 1983-84 when he joined Wakefield Trinity on a short-term contract and made a big impression at Belle Vue, but he did not stay quite long enough to make his immense presence tell. And then just to prove the South Australian cynics wrong, Wally had two spells in the newly instigated ARL, when he joined the new and very successful Brisbane Broncos club. He was a tremendous signing for them. He later had a short spell with the Gold Coast side but there were difficulties at the club and it folded after only a short life.

However, the State of Origin series was the national stage for Wally Lewis. Playing 29 times for Queensland, mostly under the coaching of another northern legend, Arthur Beetson, he led the Maroons time after time as captain and was the figurehead of the state. More than once his state's war cry, "Queenslander" was heard coming from the stand-off and also from his heart, as he forced his team-mates to deeds of unequalled valour in some of the fiercest battles ever seen on the field of play. Wally coached his beloved Queensland for the first time in 1993 but the series was lost two-one.

His skills were many and varied and his kicking game a treat to behold. His controlled short grubber kick, which split most defences, was not kicked with the foot, but perfected and practised so that the ball was propelled by dropping it onto his knee and pushing it through the onrushing defensive line.

His partnership with the outstanding scrum-half, Allan Langer, was one of the most successful in the game's history and laid the foundation of many a victory for club, state and country. I was asked by the sponsors to present the first Adidas Golden Boot award for the world's best player to Wally at the Royal Grand Hotel in Brisbane in 1985, and it was a pleasure to do so. Wally was called King Wally in Queensland and was the first player I ever saw greeted by the fans with outstretched arms and bowing.

I can even forgive him for scoring a try against my Great Britain side in the final test at Central Park in 1986 that should not have been allowed. For once in that series we came to grips with the 'Australian problem' of how to maintain a high intensity throughout the full 80 minutes of the game and going into the final quarter we were actually in front, but a penalty try given against us gave the Australians a sniff and Wally Lewis broke our hearts with a super try, side-stepping and swerving in a 25-yard run to the posts but, as the video proves, it came on the seventh tackle.

A powerful build allowed Wally to operate at loose-forward on a few occasions but it was as a stand-off half that he is remembered, a go-forward leader with superb skills and the kind of player, along with the wonderful Beetson, that Queensland is missing today. Who is there today that could issue the blood curdling call "Queenslander" that brought the best out of men - only King Wally, the hero, Lewis.

	App	Tries	Goals	Pts
Brisbane Broncos	42+4	20	11	102
Wakefield Trinity	10	6	0	24
Queensland	35	7	2	30
Australia	33	11	2	45

Also played for Brisbane Valleys, Wynnum-Manly, Fortitude Valley.

Sean Long

It is always difficult to write about those who are still involved in the game as players. For instance, what could have been a faultless career   might be scarred by an event such as the betting scandal which surrounded the two Saints stars, Sean Long and Martin Gleeson in 2004. They were found guilty of a serious breach of the game's very strict laws on players betting on the outcome of a game.

But to quote a well-used and very true adage: "There but for the grace of God, go I". I suppose it could happened to any of us, given certain circumstances. This piece, however, is about a player who is deeply involved in professional rugby league and the good things in his successful career to date. Sean Long signed for the great Wigan club in September 1993. His junior team had been Wigan St Jude's, a cracking little club operating in the North West Counties ARL.

It turned out to be a traumatic period in Sean's early career as he suffered a ruptured cruciate knee ligament and, for a time, things looked bad for the young half-back. Such an injury can curtail a player's career and Sean worked hard in his rehabilitation. It appears that the Wigan club, with Shaun Edwards, Craig Murdock and Martin Crompton available for the half-back role, considered young Long surplus to requirements, so when he had returned to fitness, Sean joined his dad, Bernard, at Widnes for a nominal transfer fee. He made the first-team scrum-half job his own at Widnes and stayed there for around two seasons until St Helens spotted the blonde-haired half-back and monitored his progress, before paying a substantial £80,000 for him.

He made his debut for Saints in 1997, four years, a career-threatening injury and another playing club, Widnes, since signing as a very promising local lad for Wigan. He settled in immediately at Knowsley Road and became a crowd-pleaser to the very demanding and knowledgeable Saints supporters. His partnership with the clever and experienced campaigner, Tommy Martyn, welded a cast-iron half-back pairing and became the envy of all the Super League clubs. The two excellent footballers had an almost telepathic communication, one seemed to know just what the other was about to do. The duo were always in the correct position to support each other, or hit one another with long passes, or chip kick for each other to run onto - in fact their combination verged on the supernatural.

The side evolved from the coaching strength of Ellery Hanley, to the steady and secure wisdom of Shaun McRae, through to the Svengali like control of Ian Millward. Giving Sean his head and allowing him to run the show on the field, Ian Millward brought the best out of the player and his accurate goalkicking became a vital match-winning facet of the Saints' game plan. At first, Chris Joynt was at loose-forward in Millward's Saints team, but with the superb signing of the world class Paul Sculthorpe, the 'eternal triangle' of Martyn, Long and Sculthorpe created an international-class quality in those vital positions. Grand Final and Challenge Cup wins came their way, the league leaders place was theirs, exciting wins against Saints' most dangerous opponents were registered, some in the final play of a match or, indeed, with the last pass of the game. Amid all this excitement the crowds rolled in to support the most enthralling team in Super League.

Suddenly the famous old club, with a reputation second-to-none, was rocked by the bad news of the betting scandal. The two players, Long and Gleeson were found guilty and both sentenced to a lengthy period of suspension. Gleeson was, in fact, transferred to Warrington. The pairing of Martyn and Long was broken well before Sean's suspension, when Tommy was allowed to take a coaching job at Leigh and the quiet, but very effective Australian, Jason Hooper, arrived to conduct another special working partnership with Sean.

Injuries to Paul Sculthorpe, plus missing Sean, cost Saints dear in the league placings in 2004 and several results went against them because of the unavailability of these key players. Sean Long remained an international class scrum-half who returned to the international scene following his comeback to the club game.

His long distance tries and his ability to pop over the crucial drop-goals are among the things I think about when discussing this chirpy character who, on reflection, has not yet completely fulfilled his obvious promise. He has so much to offer our game that when one considers his talents, one wonders why there are not more international caps in his cabinet to go with his club and international achievements. But there should be an award for courage for fighting back after his early career injury and rejection by Wigan. That itself is true heroism.

	App	Tries	Goals	Pts
Wigan	3+9	2	2	12
Widnes	8+1	2	14	35
St Helens	189+10	109	724	1,875
England	3+1	2	5	18
Great Britain	6+2	1	3	10
(To end 2004 season)				

Ken Loxton

Possibly only the rugby league connoisseur would accept that of all the world-class players in this book I would pick Ken Loxton as the best all-round player I ever coached. Consider too, with the greatest respect to Ken, that he was probably the slowest runner that I ever coached and this hindrance only adds to his prowess as a great player.

A good yardstick is to ask a player's team-mates if they rate him and again Ken's pedigree comes out. Some may ask: "Was he a better scrum-half than Alex Murphy?" Well all I can say is that Ken did things that Alex couldn't and he did them for my teams. Someone else also thought Ken was a better scrum-half than Alex, for in 1971, when playing for Huddersfield, Ken was selected over Alex as scrum-half in a test against the touring New Zealanders.

Ken also played loose-forward and again one may ask, was Loxton better than Vince Karalius? Ninety-nine out of 100 would say no. I'm the one hundredth, because for me and my teams, yes he was.

A Normanton lad, Ken learned his football, as they say around there, 'in the right area'. For many years the West Yorkshire mining villages produced great footballers and none more than the Normanton, Sharlston and Streethouse districts. In a lot of cases these young rugby league streetwise players travelled no further than Featherstone Rovers or Castleford when they signed as professionals, but some escaped the net and signed for the bigger clubs of Wakefield Trinity, Bradford Northern or even Leeds. Ken was one who moved to the traditional surroundings of great stars of the past such as Harold Wagstaff, the 'prince of centres', Dougie Clark, the Cumberland wrestling champion who won the DSM for bravery in the First World War, Albert Rosenfeld, world record try scorer over a season, Dave Valentine, the fabulous Scot who is a legend in the game and many others. This team was, of course, the superb Huddersfield club at the wonderful Fartown ground.

Ken's style was to make play for others. At Fartown, he was copied by other players, me included, and set-piece moves were named after him, 'Kenny's three' was a popular move, or a 'Locky' from a scrum was another. Frank Davies scored many tries and played for Yorkshire on the back of Ken Loxton's bravery when the latter would run across the face of a defence and slip a runner through the gap, then take an almighty clatter, usually to the head. Frank and Ken made a tremendous pair. No matter what one did to counter the Loxton moves it was virtually impossible to stop them because the man was so brave that he would still continue the move, knowing he would take a bang and to the devil with the consequences.

When rebuilding my side at Halifax in 1978, I went to Keighley for Ken and got him at a bargain price. His organisation on the field and his guts, skill and personality rubbed off on players and made them better for it. At Thrum Hall, Huddersfield's Frank Davies was effectively replaced by Dave Callan, who several times in a game would burst clean through, by way of Ken's astute handling. Ken was a copybook tackler too; I can't recall him missing one. He tackled around the legs and dropped them like felling a tree. The Halifax forwards would queue up to run off him, and the opposition, when carrying the ball would run away from him because they found it impossible to pass him.

Although at Halifax we had a very successful squad, it was a numerically small one, but there was no comfort zone, no player took it easy as they all wanted to play in a situation where the club was struggling to survive. Because of senior players like Ken, there was a no-fail feeling to each game, continuous winning became the norm, and Ken was backed up by all the squad. It was a great time to be at Halifax. When I left, Ken, along with Mick Blacker, took on the coaching job at Thrum Hall and did it well.

Two years later I was at Bramley and heard that Ken had left Halifax. I immediately asked him to join us and he did. Playing among a balanced side of good youngsters and experienced players with a lot left in them, we turned the club's fortunes around and only just missed promotion, beating Salford, one of the sides who did go up, by more than 50 points at McLaren Field. A young forward who learned much from Ken was a kid I signed from junior football called Karl Harrison.

Playing at Cardiff, Ken went in to perform one of his solid leg tackles on that superb rugby union convert, Tommy David. Both players fell down, and it was obvious both were hurt. Tommy David had broken a shin bone and Ken had damaged his spine. The Cardiff club doctor was a top orthopaedic specialist and was at the game. He phoned ahead to the hospital to get everything prepared in the theatre and operated on Ken as soon as he could.

Ken overcame that horrendous injury and coached later at Featherstone Rovers with Peter Fox. He was the best hero I ever coached.

	App	Tries	Goals	Pts
Huddersfield	207+9	14	3	48
Keighley	101+2	7	0	21
Halifax	87+19	2	0	6
Bramley	31	1	0	3
Great Britain	1	0	0	0

Keith Mason snr

If one talks to players who played in big Keith's era, they will all say "One tough bastard". That he was. Today he would be called an enforcer. He would carry the ball up all afternoon, knock any and everything down that came his way and was the champion of the young players who played in the same team as him. Nobody, but nobody, messed with the kids who played in the same team as big Keith Mason.

His career lasted longer than most and I tried to sign him at four different clubs, but without any luck.

He did come to me when I was coaching at Halifax in 1978. Keith was a tall, slim front-rower, with a reputation as a big hitter in the town of Dewsbury. He may have been short on a few skills as a youngster, but he could fight. His credentials as a front-rower, in those days of props of mammoth size, were questionable, not because of his courage or toughness, but purely because of his lack of physical bulk. So when this kid of around six-feet three-inches and 14 stones told me he was a prop, I advised him to change his position to second-row, work on his pace and I would give him a trial. He thanked me and said: "No thanks", and drifted away.

A couple of seasons later I noticed the name Mason, in the front-row at Dewsbury's Crown Flatt ground and when I saw him again I nearly died. He was around 17 stones and fit. I needed a big prop and made a bid for him, but it was refused. Fearless, even more so now he was of gargantuan proportions, Keith mixed it with the toughest props around. Les Boyd, the iron-hard Australian who sickened a few in his day, once wrote in the Warrington match day programme that big Keith was the hardest British prop he had faced here. This was after Boyd and Keith had been sent off at Warrington together for battling. As they were going into the dressing room Boyd called Keith an unacceptable name and the heavyweight from Dewsbury Moor flattened the Australian test prop in the passageway under the old stand at Wilderspool.

Keith rates Glynn 'Harry' Beverley, the former Leeds, Dewsbury, Workington and Fulham prop as one of his toughest opponents and remembers playing against him at Craven Cottage, Fulham, in 1980. Dewsbury had travelled to the capital city with a weakened side because of injuries and there were a few young kids playing against a very tough and experienced Fulham team led by player-coach Reg Bowden. True to form, Keith had protected a couple of his young team-mates from the big, bad Fulham pack, but it was impossible to stop Harry Beverley crashing over for a try late in the game.

Joining Hunslet, with David Ward as coach, Keith played the best football of his career and he formed a rousing connection at Elland Road with Sonny Nickle, Kelvin Skerrett and Australian test forward, David Gillespie, as they became one of the toughest packs in the league. Gaining promotion from the Second Division, Hunslet were unfortunate to be relegated the following season and the good side fragmented.

Keith went into amateur coaching and did very well with a pub team, The Crown. Winning all the cups possible to them in their league, the little side had good runs in the Yorkshire Cup and the BARLA National Cup and were a very hard team to beat on their own midden. The story was that his team, The Crown, dare not lose, and the opposition dare not win when Keith was prowling on the touchline. But the story is untrue for Keith is really a soft-hearted hard-case, a decent bloke for a former tough front-rower.

Keith junior, his son, is a good forward, still a young man, and already an international player having represented Wales, A big lad, like his dad, Keith junior, started his professional career at Wakefield Wildcats, then moved out to Australia to play for the Melbourne Storm club before being signed by St Helens and was a member of their 2004 Challenge Cup winning side.

Keith also rates the original 'Maori Warrior', Kevin Tamati as a tough opponent and reckons that the Warrington front row of that time, the mid-1980s, Boyd, Tamati and another Australian, Bob Jackson, as possibly the toughest he ever grappled with. In fact, Kevin Tamati was overheard top say, after Keith's spat with Les Boyd: "I advised Les not to mix it with big Mason as I had seen this guy in action before." So this thin kid from my Halifax days had matured into a big, strong front rower who could play and 'scrap' a bit.

Keith never played in a Challenge Cup final, and neither has he a cupboard full of medals. What he gained in our game was the respect of the players he battled with and the life long thanks of the kids he protected. He is well thought of in rugby league and it is always a pleasure to meet up with him and talk about the old days when he was a thin youngster. Because now he is a big fat hero.

	App	Tries	Goals	Pts
Dewsbury	115+20	3	0	12
Hunslet	80+2	1	0	4

Brian McTigue

No record of my heroes would be complete without mention of Brian McTigue. Brian figured in almost every forward position for Wigan at some time or other in his long and distinguished career wearing the famous cherry and white jersey. In his early years at the club he was a second-row forward, occasionally playing at number 13. As Brian stiffened out in physique, he moved to the front-row and that is where he is remembered for producing some memorable and sterling displays both in club, county and international football.

His background as a youngster was from the hard mining environment of the Lancashire coalfields and his persona on the playing field was just that, tough, no-nonsense, uncompromising, no quarter asked nor given, iron hard but perhaps surprisingly, he was a very skilful ball-handler. His defence was unshakeable, he would stop a runner dead in his tracks with a full-blooded bodycheck and a shattering tackle. He had been a boxer of some note as a younger sportsman and having trained for that particularly hard sport in mind and body, could handle himself in what is accepted as the hardest team sport in the world.

For any newcomer to our game, or a youngster reading this, it may be useful to explain the variations between the game today and then. Before Super League, and possibly up to about the late 1960s and early 1970s, our game had not evolved much since the breakaway from rugby union in 1895 and the development of the basic rugby league rules. Since then, we have had rule changes that had enhanced the game. The protection of players is far better these days with the spear tackle outlawed, flopping with knees in the tackle, the 'grapple tackle', where the neck is twisted around in a wrestling hold have all been stopped. However, the downright brutality of the game as it was then was hard to believe without having seen or played it.

Punching in the scrum is rarely seen these days, thank goodness, and head-butting in the pack is also very rare. One must remember too that taking an opponent out of the game was considered tactical in the past, so it helped a player considerably if he could look after himself. Brian McTigue was, as well as being a great ball-playing forward, was one of the best at looking after himself. In the piece on Clive Churchill earlier in this book, I mentioned that the great man had described Brian's assault on Ian Walsh, the Australian hooker, as "the most despicable act I ever saw in a test match", but that kind of action was common then. It was second nature to dispatch an opponent as quickly as possible, especially if he was, like Walsh, a great ball-winner. Tackles were higher, fighting between players was more common, cuts and stitches were seen more often and the obligatory cauliflower ear was noticed more than today.

I recall, as a spectator, the first round Challenge Cup tie between Leeds and Wigan in 1957. In a nail-biter of a cup tie, Brian was involved, at some time or another, with most of the Leeds pack and in the thick of the action. With five minutes to play, the fearsome, red-haired Leeds prop, Joe Anderson, who was a hard case himself, suddenly went down after a clash with Brian and was carried off with what was described later as concussion.

Brian was no respecter of reputations and the Australians hated playing against him. They would queue up to take a pop at him, but he saw them all off. Almost every player, back or forward, who played with or against him and to whom I have spoken over my years in the game, say without hesitation that the three hardest men they played against were Stan Owen of Leigh, Derek Turner of Wakefield Trinity and Brian McTigue.

Brian toured in 1958 and 1962 and played in the famous win in Brisbane in 1958, when tour captain Alan Prescott played almost the whole of the test with a broken arm. Brian played in four of the five tests on that tour and the two in New Zealand he was at open-side prop against the bull-like Maori, Joe Ratima. The two winning tests he played against the Australians on that tour were at blind-side prop and both against the tough Balmain number 10, Bill Marsh.

Brian gained 25 Great Britain caps between 1958 and 1963 and Lancashire honours. His medal count with Wigan includes those won in the Challenge Cup, Lancashire Cup, Championship and Lancashire League winners, plus a similar list of runners-up medals.

Whenever an expert pencils in his best ever side, McTigue is frequently in it, somewhere in the pack. I can see now the thinning hair and those powerfully strong legs and arms. Standing in a tackle, the ball held like a tennis ball in one huge hand and being flicked away in a superb pass to a team mate, is another vision I have of him. And I recall him standing his ground also and knocking over those big Australian forwards in the tackle when he was defending. With all five tests under his belt on the 1962 tour and another Ashes win, he is another hero

	App	Tries	Goals	Pts
Wigan	422	44	3	138
Blackpool Borough	1	0	0	0
Lancashire	11	2	0	6
Great Britain	25	2	0	6

Roger Millward MBE

While in hospital in 1964, I followed the fortunes of a young stand-off half, who was representing his town in a televised inter-town competition at under-17 level. The player was the excellent Roger Millward, who went on to great things in a career that moved through playing into an equally successful coaching period. But this young prodigy, born in Castleford in September 1947, although signing for his hometown club in September 1964, was destined not to make his name at Wheldon Road, now known as The Jungle, but 60 miles due east, at the famous Craven Park, the long-time home of Hull Kingston Rovers.

Snapped up on his 17th birthday, Roger was seen at Castleford as the natural successor to either Alan Hardisty or Keith Hepworth, the brilliant H bombs of the up-and-coming young Castleford side. But because of the international standard form of the H bombs, both were test players, Roger found it almost impossible to win a regular place in that side. He played now and again, making his debut at Dewsbury in October 1964, but in the big matches, if fit, both Hardisty and Hepworth were in, and Roger, despite his brilliance, was out. This could not continue and in August 1966, Roger was transferred to Hull KR for the tidy sum of £6,000. The shrewd directors at Craven Park saw the young Millward as the lynchpin in their plans to build a team to challenge their arch enemies across the city, Hull FC.

'Roger the Dodger', as he was known throughout the game, made his Hull KR debut at Hunslet on 15 August 1966. His signing had an immediate impact as Hull KR moved up the league, becoming a power in the game. His influence was seen with Yorkshire Cup wins in 1966-67 and 1967-68. After he became captain of the side in 1969, the club recorded further victories in the county cup in 1971-72 and 1974-75. His crowning glory, after being appointed player-coach in March 1977 was the much admired successful Challenge Cup campaign of 1980.

Roger had been a hero for quite a few years by 1980, but he was without a Wembley appearance. The media was excited at the prospect of two likely events that year in the Challenge Cup Final. One was the strong possibility of an all-Hull final and the second that Roger would make his long-awaited appearance there because Hull KR had drawn Second Division Halifax in the semi-final, where I was the coach. Hull KR were one of the First Division's strongest teams, packed full of international players, so it was a good bet that they would reach Wembley. Hull FC beat Widnes in the other semi, Hull KR beat us and the way was open for a sports-writers' extravaganza.

The legend of that final began on the Friday morning before the match with the hand-painted sign, driven into the grass verge at the beginning of the Hull end of the M62, which read: "Will the last one out, please turn off the lights?" It had a fairytale end as the great Roger Millward lifted the old cup after a wonderful 10-5 victory.

His long and successful term at Craven Park ended in May 1991 when he joined Halifax as coach. Not long after this he left Thrum Hall, in December 1992, a disillusioned and disappointed man. His career had been one of total success and life at Halifax was so different to what he had expected. Roger made 29 appearances for Great Britain in test and World Cup matches and captained the national side 10 times. He toured on three Lions trips and had a total of six international visits to Australia and New Zealand, with two World Cups in 1968 and 1977 and as captain of England in the 1975 World Championship competition. He played 17 times for England, skippering them in 13 of those matches. Roger also captained Yorkshire and gained 12 county caps. One of his cherished records is that he played in four positions in international rugby league: stand-off, scrum-half, centre and on the wing.

The highlight of his Lions tours was the Ashes win of 1970. In the second test in Sydney, with the tourists one test down, Roger took the Australians to the cleaners when he recorded two tries and seven goals for a record-equalling 20 point haul. In the final test, with the Australians coming back and Great Britain only one point in front, Roger took a superb Doug Laughton pass to slice through the Australian defence for the winner - a wonderful try.

Roger scored a record 207 tries for Hull KR, 16 for Castleford, 17 for Great Britain, three for England, eight for Yorkshire, one for Great Britain under-24s and 27 on his three tours in games other than tests, giving him a total of 279 tries. He has a career total of 718 goals, plus 10 drop-goals, giving a grand total of 2,283 points.

He was one of the smallest men ever to tour or play for Great Britain, Roger played with his brains and skill. He was very quick off the mark and blessed with a superb sidestep. Roger proved that if you're good enough, you're big enough. Small man, huge hero.

	App	**Tries**	**Goals**	**Pts**
Castleford	34+6	16	35	118
Hull KR	400+7	207	617	1,825
Yorkshire	12	8	22	68
Great Britain	28+1	17	15	81
England	16+1	3	10	29

Ces Mountford MBE

What an age it was for stand-off halves in this country from 1946 to 1953. If the princes were Dickie Williams, Ron Rylance, Willie Horne, Ken Dean and Ray Price, then the prince regent was Willie Davies and the king was New Zealander, Ces Mountford. What days too at Central Park, and without detracting from the outstanding side of the late 1980s and early 1990s, this team, from the end of the Second World War to the middle 1950s and beyond, were the best in the land. Their star-filled, wonderful backs were given great spaces to run into by a hard-working and fine supporting pack of forwards and, as in all class orchestras, a brilliant conductor was required. That man was Ces Mountford.

Ces fetched and carried, made and scored tries, marshalled and moved his team around the field and did everything except cut the oranges at half-time. He played at a time when certain positions were the real glamorous places to be: stand-off half, loose-forward, wingman and centre were the Hollywood positions, and Ces was a fabulous leading man. He arrived on these shores unsung and, with respect, virtually unknown. It is hard to believe, but Ces never represented his beloved New Zealand as a player. In 1939 every man and his dog on the South Island considered Ces a certainty to make that year's Kiwi tour to Great Britain because he had starred for both his club side, Blackball and his district side, West Coast, all season. Everyone thought he must make the ship, except the North Island-orientated selectors, who gave the excuse that they considered him too young at 17.

The ill-fated tour lasted only two games after war was declared and the Kiwis had to get back home quickly. So the love affair between Ces and the Wigan club and its supporters started when the stocky little master burst onto the post-war scene and, on 31 August 1946, he made his debut for the cherry and whites against the tough tackling Belle Vue Rangers at the famous Belle Vue complex in Manchester. From this beginning a superb story of hard work and ultimate success is told in his autobiography, *Kiwis, Wigan and The Wire*.

As a youngster in 1946 and, even by that time, an ardent Leeds supporter, the game I always looked forward to was Wigan's visit to Headingley. My Dad worked on the railways and he could get reduced price tickets to almost anywhere, so we would travel to watch Leeds play away and I was lucky to be able to attend matches in Lancashire, notably at Central Park.

No matter how well Ces Mountford played against Leeds, it didn't bother me, because his artistry and skill took precedence and even at that age I knew I was watching a top class player. That is except for one instance when we went to Wigan in September 1949. Leeds were having the better of the game when the much-feared Ces was injured early in the second half. Because there were no substitutes then, Ces, limping heavily, took his place on the wing to maintain 13 players on the field for the home side. With the threat of Mountford out of the way, Leeds looked to have the match won because well into injury time they held a 12-10 lead. There was one scrum left, one tackle to make to complete a brilliant win at Central Park. Wigan won the scrum and Ces drifted infield to take makeshift stand-off Ernie Ashcroft's pass and slice between Leeds's Kiwi centre, Ike Procter and stand-off Dickie Williams. Selling the perfect dummy, Ces hit the gap between the two Leeds players and left Procter grasping at air. Williams turned and gave chase only a yard behind. I always thought Kiwis couldn't fly. This one did, head back, knowing that the try line was approaching and Williams, head down, chasing for all he was worth. The rocket-propelled Mountford crashed over the line, with Williams inches behind him, for a glorious, winning touchdown and, as Ces was mobbed by his team mates, nobody booed louder than me at the sight of this injured player being swamped by delighted players in cherry and white.

The *Yorkshire Evening Post* called it "foul play" and a "dirty trick", but it was in fact a Mountford special, a try that I was fortunate to witness, and having seen that try and also being at Central Park to see Bert Cook kick his monster goal three years earlier in the famous cup win by Leeds, I was indeed blessed.

Those of us still around who can recall Ces and his terrific skills are indeed lucky to remember one of the all-time great players. We also recall him as a coach who gained the respect of everyone he worked with, and those who were coached by him on his journeys around New Zealand with his travelling coaching school. We were delighted to see a New Zealand, Wigan and Warrington legend and hero, making it, at last, as the New Zealand international coach.

	App	Tries	Goals	Pts
Wigan	210	70	55	320
Warrington	37	6	2	22
Other Nationalities	5	0	0	0

Also played for Blackball, West Coast

Alex Murphy OBE

Described by many good judges of the game as the best rugby league player ever, Murph was at home in either of the half-back positions, but such was his ability and charisma, that he could have played at prop forward and performed brilliantly. He appeared on the scene at Knowsley Road like a comet. He suddenly was there, from nowhere, a brilliant star and still a teenager.

So easily did the skills and fame come to him, and such was his gift, that people mistook it for arrogance. He was exceptionally quick, his kicking was long and accurate, his ability to open a defence with a pass was awesome, he was strongly built and his defence was strong too, his step away from the tackler was allied with an unbelievable speed off the mark, he was ultra confident and he was unbearably cocky.

With respect to Alex I'll repeat an old story. Vince Karalius, the great loose-forward for Saints and Great Britain, one of the hardest of hard men, got hold of Alex in the dressing room before a home game and said: "Do me a favour if you score as usual today. Don't go over the line by going under the posts, just in case your head jams between the uprights". That was the young, brash rising star that became one of our game's biggest legends. When chosen to tour in 1958, he was the youngest ever tourist and he was pitched in against the Australian test side that included the redoubtable Keith Holman, then considered the best scrum half in the world. Murph matched him try-for-try in the three match series, and the *Sydney Sun* newspaper carried a statement from Holman, in answer to a journalist's question: "How did you rate young Murphy?" "A brilliant prospect, but Jeez, he's a cheeky little bastard," was Keith Holman's measured reply.

His crafty play and reading of the game forced a change in the laws, in the 1966 Saints versus Wigan Wembley Challenge Cup Final. In cahoots with Tommy Bishop, their persistent off-side at play-the-balls resulted in continual scrums following penalties awarded to Wigan. With Wigan kicking their penalties to touch, Saints were more likely to win the subsequent scrums as Wigan did not have a regular hooker in their team. After this final, the tap penalty following a successful penalty kick to touch was introduced.

Murph's move into coaching was as successful as his playing career and after leaving Saints he went as player-coach to Hilton Park, Leigh to be involved in one of the most controversial incidents in Wembley history in the 1971 final against Leeds. Immense underdogs Leigh gave the star-studded Leeds one heck of a run around and, mainly through frustration, Syd Hynes the Leeds international centre was seen to aim a punch at Murph that appeared to miss him by a mile. Murph went down as if poleaxed and referee Billy Thompson had no option but to send off Hynes, who became the first player ever to be sent off at Wembley. What infuriated the Leeds supporters was that Leigh won the final 24-7 and Murph, who had been carried off on a stretcher, came back as large as life to accept his medal and the cup at the end of the game, apparently unscathed.

He then moved to Warrington and built up a very good, hard side at Wilderspool and returned to Wembley in 1974 to win the Cup against Featherstone Rovers 24-9, before reaching the final again in 1975, this time losing to Widnes, 14-7. Spells as coach at Salford and Leigh again, where he won the First Division Championship in 1982, were followed by the plum job at Wigan, taking over from me. After a stint as coach at his first love, St Helens, then came a complete shift in levels as he took over at lower-league Huddersfield in the 1991-92 season. That season I was coaching at Bramley and both our teams won promotion from the old Third Division.

Alex Murphy made his name at St Helens as a brilliant player with, as my Dad used to say, "more edge than a broken teapot". Because of this, the majority of the Wigan supporters after begrudgingly accepting his appointment as coach to their club, but some turned against him as time went by and results worsened, causing him to walk away from the job. But this was only after they had won the Regal Trophy in 1983, beating Leeds 15-4 at Elland Road, and reached Wembley in 1984, losing to Widnes 19-6.

Alex won 27 international caps with Great Britain and did just about everything a player can do in the game. In coaching his success rate is second to none, with Challenge Cup Finals, Championships, Lancashire Cup successes as well as coaching England in the World Championship in 1975. He missed out on the ultimate coaching job, that of Great Britain, I think because of politics and possibly because of standing on a few toes as a player and a coach earlier in his career but, with what he achieved in the game, I imagine he can live with that.

Make no mistake, Alex Murphy, love him or hate him, was one of the top three ever to play this game at the top level. A true hero of heroes.

	App	Tries	Goals	Pts
St Helens	319	175	42	609
Leigh	113+5	33	96	291
Warrington	66+1	9	40	107
Lancashire	14	12	2	40
Great Britain	27	16	0	48
England	2	1	1	5

Frank O'Rourke and Jeff Moores

Two for the price of one. Both these young Australians were recommended to Leeds at a time when the club needed an injection of personalities into the side. Without a Yorkshire Cup win since 1921-22, and a Challenge Cup Final win since 1923, the Leeds public wanted a star or two to cheer on those cold wintry afternoons at Headingley and the start of the 1927-28 season was near.

Frank O'Rourke

But to set the scene one must understand how the Leeds club operated when attempting to sign a player from Australia. Leeds had signed a centre on recommendation, from Penrith at the foot of the Blue Mountains, inland from Sydney. Dinny Campbell was a very good middle back. He had nine successful seasons at Headingley before returning home and went with the good wishes of the Leeds supporters and the board of directors, and was asked to look out for any talented backs who may be looking for an English club when the current ban on Dominion players was set to be lifted in 1927. Campbell did just that and following his recommendation a cablegram was sent by Mr George Ibbotson of Leeds to Dinny to make a "tentative offer" to O'Rourke of £700 as a transfer fee, one second-class return fare and a position in the scholastic profession, plus playing terms of £6 for a win, £4 for a draw

Jeff Moores

and £3 for a loss. Not bad for 1926-27. Mr Ibbotson ended the cablegram with a prophetic addendum: "We also require a class stand-off half".

Frank O'Rourke accepted the terms and Dinny Campbell cabled Mr Ibbotson describing O'Rourke, while playing for the University of Sydney as "the legitimate successor to H. H. Dally Messenger". The cable to say that Leeds wanted O'Rourke was dated 6 December 1926. Then between Christmas 1926 and July 1927, Dinny Campbell targeted 'the best stand-off in Australia', a Queenslander by the name of Jeff Moores.

Moores was a tremendous player who, at the ripe old age of 22, was such an influence on the Leeds team when he arrived that he was made captain. A naturally skilful footballer and above all a fierce competitor, Moores's stand-up-and-knock-'em-over defensive style was something the Leeds faithful had only dreamed about for years. But before the signing was finalised, another cablegram from Mr Ibbotson read: "Agree to pay Moore the same as O'Rourke if he is prepared to accept immediately and sail at same time. Sending O'Rourke's money tomorrow. Cable Moores's reply and his address". So the arrival of the two most influential middle backs that Leeds had had for years was awaited with relish. The two men were slightly different in background but not in style as O'Rourke, the polished university teacher and Moores, the bush kid from the sticks, both played the game harder than most.

Frank made his debut in September 1927 and his robust style of both attack and defence made him an instant favourite with the Leeds crowd who loved both these fresh-faced young players from so far away. O'Rourke's hard, straight running had the big Leeds crowds on their feet and the strong, tough schoolteacher was great value for money as he gave 100 per cent in the time he spent at Leeds before returning home to accept an important job in education in December 1933. He played 240 games for the club and scored 122 tries as well as stopping at least the same amount with his daredevil tackling.

Jeff Moores, the superb stand-off or centre who made such a difference to the Leeds club's attitude to winning, can also be regarded as a recruiter in the mould of Campbell, because on his return from a trip home in 1930, he brought back a player who became a bigger legend at Leeds than himself: Eric Harris, the 'Toowoomba Ghost'.

For the next three years Jeff nursed and nurtured and looked after Harris like a younger brother and it was Moores's skill that helped to develop the career of the finest wingman Leeds ever signed.

But at the start of the 1933-34 season Jeff Moores was exchanged for York's very fast Sep Aspinall and a tremendous period ended as Leeds lost both O'Rourke and Moores within months of each other. Rumours abound over why Jeff was sent to York in the prime of his career, some said that he had argued with the board of directors over a few pounds expenses which in those days of strict club discipline, would have been enough to cause the club to sack even Jeff Moores. He continued for a few seasons with York and finally went home to Australia leaving a final testimony of his love of the Leeds club in the able, slim shape of his mate from Brisbane Wests, Eric Harris.

How come O'Rourke and Moores are heroes of mine even though they left the Leeds club before I was born? Well, I was brought up on tales of derring-do by my Dad in stories of extreme heroism by these two and more Leeds rugby league heroes. That's why they are mine.

Frank O'Rourke

	App	Tries	Goals	Pts
Leeds	240	122	9	384

Also played for University of New South Wales.

Jeff Moores

	App	Tries	Goals	Pts
Leeds	211	98	24	342
York	154	40	7	134

Also played for Brisbane Wests, Queensland.

Jonathan 'Jonty' Parkin

Of all the larger-than-life characters who have graced our game over the years, Jonty Parkin ranks with the best. He was the king-pin player of his time, an Alex Murphy of the old game, in fact he 'out-Murphied' Murphy.

While this piece is about the fabulous Jonty Parkin, a simple comparison between these two fantastic players in two vastly different ages is worthwhile. Both were brilliant tacticians, strong defenders, excellent kickers and above all, both were born leaders who led from the front. Their international careers were similar, the stories about them are similar too and both were outstanding characters in the game.

Jonty was a Sharlston lad, born and bred. Not many clubs were without a player from this superb nursery of young natural talent as my piece on Herbert Goodfellow points out. The grand old Sharlston club play on the same ground today that saw the growth of Parkin and Goodfellow.

Jonty signed for Wakefield Trinity in 1913, aged just 17. His debut game was played in Lancashire, but his home debut on his beloved Belle Vue was in November 1913, against the tough St Helens side. The First World War took its toll of Trinity players and at the resumption of the league, a complete rebuild of the side was required. However, they had a wonderful base with Jonty as their star half-back. In 1920 he earned the first of his 17 Great Britain caps, against Australia in Brisbane. Although from 1918 through to 1924 Wakefield were a hard team to beat, not much silverware decorated the boardroom. However, 1924 saw a Yorkshire Cup Final win against a strong Batley side.

As captain of the Lions on his second tour of duty in 1924, Jonty resumed his successful partnership with that other legend of the West Riding, Frank Gallagher, who, if not at stand-off as Jonty's partner, was at loose-forward to cover the maestro at half-back. Touring again in 1928 as captain, Jonty's third tour, he suffered an injury that meant he played in only two of the six tests.

In all three of his tours, Jonty played in 11 of a possible 18 tests which is testimony to his toughness and durability. For many years he captained Trinity, Yorkshire and Great Britain, a tremendous honour for a lad from a small village and the people of Sharlston must have been very proud of their famous son. Receiving only a pittance when signing in 1913, Jonty was granted a benefit match in 1922. He chose the well-supported game against Leeds as the match for his fund-raising and the princely sum of £700 was the gate receipts, a substantial benefit in those austere days.

As well as his Great Britain and Yorkshire caps, Jonty also collected 12 England caps. However, his prowess as a player did not end with scoring tries and kicking goals. He was a thinker, a student of the game and a man who, because of his ability on the field, was courted by controversy for most of his superb career, just like Alex Murphy. In one Yorkshire Cup game at Headingley in 1924, Leeds were winning 4-2 and Trinity were awarded a penalty kick. The attempt went wide of the posts and the ball was caught in the in-goal area by Syd Walmsley, the Leeds full-back who, without touching the ball on the ground to make it dead, threw the ball forward to Jim Bacon to drop-kick out as usual to restart play. Jonty was on to the mistake in a flash and complained to the referee, who supported his claim for a forward pass. From the ensuing scrum near the Leeds try line, Jonty forced his way over for the winning try. This raised the anger of the Leeds public to a fever pitch.

After considering Jonty to be too old for international rugby in 1929, the selectors left him out of the first test against the Australians and Great Britain lost. They brought him back for the next two and Great Britain won. They were his last two international appearances, but he had a final trick up his sleeve. In 1930, the Wakefield committee decided to transfer list Jonty and asked a £100 fee for him. The unheard of happened: Jonty paid the £100 and bought himself. He said he didn't want any other club to have "any hassle in signing me". A free agent, he signed for Hull KR in September 1930 and graced Craven Park for two final years. Only Jonty (or Alex) would have done that. He did go back to Wakefield in 1947, when he was voted onto the club committee and loved the association again with his Trinity club.

So died the legend in 1972. Brilliant is an inadequate word for this all time hero.

	App	Tries	Goals	Pts
Wakefield Trinity	349	96	94	476
Hull KR	57	11	27	87
Yorkshire	17	8	2	28
Great Britain	17	9	0	27
England	12	6	5	28

Keith Senior

Today's heroes are no lesser men than players of my era and it would be remiss of me to leave out a player of such obvious talents as Keith. I have admired his playing ability for quite a few seasons now and the one thing that attracts me to those talents is that he is one of the few British players who has performed consistently well against all the big countries in international matches. Keith is a big man: six-feet three-inches tall and weighing in at around 16 stones. He is unmissable not only because of his size, but also because of his shaved head. He signed for Sheffield Eagles from the Huddersfield YMCA rugby union club in 1994 as an 18-year-old. He quickly made his mark and was soon drafted into the Eagles first team, and became a regular member.

Keith is an exciting runner and a strong defender. The Leeds Rhinos supporters love nothing better than to see Keith tearing down his left-hand side channel in full flight. Speaking to several players who play against him regularly in Super League, they all bear testimony to his speed off the mark for a big man and his ability to manoeuvre the would-be tackler into a position from where Keith accelerates and leaves them helpless. His sheer size helps a lot too as, together with his bulk, he has power. Another of his attacking qualities is his hand-off plus, at the same time, a swerve that takes him clear of the tackler.

His international debut was against the Kiwis in New Zealand in 1996. He is a scorer of important tries in big matches and this gift was seen in good light when he stormed over for the crucial try for England in the quarter-final of the 2000 World Cup against Ireland.

Virtually ever-present since 1998 for Great Britain, he is respected by both Australian and New Zealand players. His strength and football ability are recognised by the experts as Keith has held his centre position in the annual expert-selected World XIII for the two years of 2002 and 2003, no mean feat for an English player today.

For all his successes at Headingley and his sterling performances for England and Great Britain though, the crowning moment of his career must have been when, as a Sheffield Eagles player, he was a member of the side that went into the history books as the team with no chance which beat odds-on favourites Wigan, at Wembley, to lift the Challenge Cup in 1998. Coached by John Kear, the Eagles, with a team of unknowns who were very much the underdogs, followed a perfect game plan to surprise everyone in the rugby league world.

The man who founded Sheffield Eagles, later the chief executive at Leeds Rhinos, Gary Hetherington, was quick to snap up the powerful finisher and in 1999 Keith made his debut for the blue and amber Rhinos against London Broncos at Headingley on the day he signed.

Always at the peak of fitness, another big plus the Rhinos get from Senior is that he is a very durable player, one who can take a knock and recover quickly, and his superb fitness levels allow him to play regularly and miss few matches. Being tall gives Keith the edge when jumping for high kicks and the current Leeds ploy of kicking to the corners, we find that when it is to the side that Senior is playing, he regains more than his share of possession from these high kicks and ultimately scores many tries from this set move.

He is also a proud Yorkshireman and has represented his county, at the time of writing, on four occasions, scoring four tries. The Leeds club has had a series of top class centres down the years, Garry Schofield, Syd Hynes, Lewis Jones, Keith McLellan, Gareth Price, Craig Innes, Kevin Iro, Andrew Ettingshausen, Mark McGaw, Bob Bartlett, Jeff Moores, Frank O'Rourke, Dinny Campbell, Fred Harris, Stanley Brogden and many, many more but Keith Senior must rate with the best. His Great Britain and England caps, Yorkshire appearances, his 140 appearances, including nine as a substitute for Sheffield and his, to date, 161 games for the Rhinos tells the story of a very, very good player. His total of 149 career tries, again to date, is not as high as some of the old-time legends but in today's game it is as good as any.

A final yardstick that makes a hero of Keith Senior is that the media loves him. An ordinary player is usually ignored by the media, that's a rule in life, but Senior has that match-winning way about his game and if the score is tight with nothing between the teams and Keith Senior is on your team, then you have a wonderful chance of winning. That is why he is a hero.

	App	Tries	Goals	Pts
Sheffield Eagles	131+9	56	0	224
Leeds Rhinos	160+1	82	0	328
Yorkshire	4	4	0	16
Great Britain	19+2	6	0	24
England	5	1	0	4
(To end 2004 season)				

Mick Shoebottom

If a fictional motion picture were to be made on the life of a professional rugby league player, then the producer would need to look no further than Mick Shoebottom for inspiration because his life contained all the requirements of a box-office smash hit and an Academy award winner. It would include humour, pathos and action with, unfortunately, a sad ending.

Mick became a legend at Headingley and as he extended his experience, pace and power in the transition from boy to man, so too his toughness and reputation as a 'hard man' grew. Mick joined the Leeds club as a youngster from the tough Leeds and District League side, Bison Sports. His older brother, George, was a second-row forward for Doncaster and although Mick was quick enough, there was a doubt over his best position because he was a slim youth.

His debut for Leeds was against Doncaster, at Headingley on 24 February 1962 and he marked the occasion with a try. A happy type of youngster, Mick was a good dressing-room player. But his nature hid a very, very tough inner self, a winner in every way while outwardly he was easy going with an infectious, positive outlook. His earliest rugby league, as a junior, was played at the famous Hunslet Boys Club and one would expect nothing less from a Hunslet born-and-bred lad.

Fair haired and good-looking, Mick gradually built up into a fine, strong athlete with a powerful burst who was very quick indeed. He had to wait for another full season after his successful debut before regular first team football came his way as he made four appearances in 1961-62 and only 10 in 1962-63, but after that he was away and winning on a wonderful, albeit sadly shortened, career.

International selection was achieved in 1968 when he went to Australia and New Zealand with the British team in the World Cup series. Earlier that year, Mick had figured in the infamous 'Watersplash' Challenge Cup Final at Wembley when Leeds beat Wakefield Trinity 11-10 in a cloudburst.

Mick was also a key player in the successful 1970 Lions tour of Australia and New Zealand where he played at full-back and centre in the three test matches against Australia. To say that there has never been a more big-hearted, honest or braver player in our game is a huge statement, but many players and former players have uttered this same statement. 'Shoey' was a one-off – a nice kid, tough as teak, a terrific competitor, quick, strong and with a reputation of being a hard player that many in the game can endorse.

In his 288 appearances for Leeds he scored 117 tries and kicked 52 goals for the club. He won 12 caps for Great Britain and several for his county, Yorkshire.

The tragic ending began on 1 May 1971 when Leeds were involved in the Championship semi-final against Salford at Headingley. It should have been a showcase game, because Salford were the big-spenders with a star-studded side and, in David Watkins and Colin Dixon, had two of the best Welsh internationals. The Leeds side was enjoying a great season, already through to the Challenge Cup Final in two weeks time against underdogs, Leigh.

Leeds were at full strength and began the match well, taking an early lead and the game ebbed and flowed in superbly sunny weather - a perfect end-of-season match. Suddenly, Shoey was striding through a gap from a great Bill Ramsey pass. Up the North Stand touchline he sprints, away from the old dressing rooms, with Colin Dixon covering across like a good loose-forward should. Dixon could run, make no mistake, and the action turned into a pure race between one fast player and another. The excellent, brave Leeds man never flinched from his duty, that of scoring for his team, as he and Dixon raced stride for stride to the corner flag and with one final heart-stopping effort Mick hurled his body over for a fine try. Colin Dixon also made one last desperate lunge and as the referee, Mr Harry Hunt, signalled for the try, from that flurry of bodies only one regained his feet. Mick Shoebottom lay, unmoving, and seriously injured.

He never played again, a severe head injury ending a super career and, in time, the life of a very brave and talented young player at 26 years of age. It was sad, too, for the totally shattered Colin Dixon who had to live with the accident. Good judges reckon that the loss of Mick Shoebottom was a blow to our international side from which it never quite recovered. He was a 100 per cent player who never took a backward step and a wholehearted man who asked, and gave, no quarter. Mick Shoebottom died in October 2002. He was a hero at Leeds before his dreadful injury, now he is a legend, a true hero.

	App	Tries	Goals	Pts
Leeds	288	117	52	455
Yorkshire	4+4	1	1	5
Great Britain	12	1	0	3

Eric Simms

When one talks of South Sydney full-backs, the name Clive Churchill always crops up. This is because Churchill was arguably the best in the world in his day. But Souths have had many fine full-backs and Eric Simms was one of those excellent players. A kicker of great repute, Eric was an Aborigine, born near Newcastle in 1945 and taught the art of goal and field-kicking by his school sportsmaster, Mr Les Leggatt. As a 19-year-old truck driver, he was given a chance to play for South Sydney and took his chance with both hands and feet as well, as Eric became Souths' goalkicker from his debut.

Australia and Souths majestic loose-forward, Ron Coote remembers Eric as a wonder goalkicker: "He was brilliant at the kicking job because he practiced it for hour after hour. Eric would be practising his goal and drop-kicking skills when we arrived for training and when we had finished, he would stay out with Clive Churchill and kick for another hour. The man had a phenomenal long and short-range kick on him and I can't ever remember him missing one. Of course he will have done, but I can't remember it."

Eric was a stocky, strong-running player with a powerful defence. Looking like a body-builder with his thick-set neck and shoulders, the power for his long-range conversions came from his perfect timing and those strong muscular legs. He was also 'Joe Cool' in matches, laid-back and unruffled by pressure. As a club player Eric played in five Grand Finals on the trot from 1967 to 1971, winning four and losing one, to Balmain in 1969.

His international career was a strange one to say the least. He represented Australia in two World Cup series only, in 1968 in Australia and in 1970 in England. Why he was never selected for his country in other than World Cup games is a mystery because his potential as a match-winner was there for all to see with his kicking alone. Simms supports Coote's theory of why Eric was such a good kicker but adds that it was helped by 'mucking around' on the Souths' ground at Redfern Oval. "Blokes would say can you kick one from here, or one from there, and I would, just for the fun of it. It sure did help me in practice," said Simms.

The drop-goal was also a big weapon in Eric's armament and his deadly accurate boot still holds the record of 86 drop-goals in a career in Australia. Eric said that practice was easy, it was doing it with tacklers flying at him in full-blooded matches with hit-men waiting their opportunity to clobber him in the act of kicking that was the problem. Eric

Simms was partly responsible for the drop-goal being reduced from being worth two points to one point in the 1971 season because he had scored 20 in the previous season.

In the 1968 World Cup, Eric scored 50 points out of the total of 113 scored by the whole Australian team. This was as many as the entire England team scored in the whole competition and more than the combined New Zealand and French teams scored.

He was a points-scoring sensation in the Sydney league too, because he scored tries as well as goals. Operating at stand-off and centre as well as at full-back for Souths, Eric scored 235 points from 24 games in 1967 and 241 points in 1970 which gave him the record for points-in-a-season in Sydney. That record was broken by Parramatta's fabulous Mick 'The Crow' Cronin in 1978 and again by the Canterbury Bulldogs marksman, Hazem El Masri in 2003. But his most remarkable feat was in 1969, when Souths travelled to Penrith Park late in the season, with Eric chasing 200 points as a personal milestone. He passed that benchmark with a towering touchline conversion of second-rower Gary Stevens's try then, with the 200 points in the pouch, in an amazing 11 minutes he kicked five drop-goals. Ron Coote takes up the story: "He could not go wrong, it was his day, his moment of glory that makes all those hours of grinding practice worth while. I remember him taking a pass some 45 yards out from the posts and bang, over it went. The second and third were almost stopped by whatever means were available to Penrith and I swear that both goals went over after sailing between the legs of the blockers bang, bang. I think fourth was a left-foot kick, he could do anything in this spell, and his final one of the five was from the halfway line, the best exhibition of kicking ever seen in Australia."

Eric went into a player-coach job at Crookwell in 1975 and a final coaching position at La Perouse until 1979. Now he works on the wharves at Port Botany. This excellent footballer will be remembered for his ability to kick the football, but his team-mates will remember him as a player who could and did score points and win games for them. League games or cup ties came the same to Eric Simms, an Aboriginal hero.

	App	Tries	Goals	Pts
South Sydney	206	23	889	1,841
Australia	1968 & 1970 World Cups			

Peter Sterling

Peter Sterling was one of the long line of top half-backs that rolled off the Australian production line and into the record books as being a member of both unbeaten Kangaroo sides who toured Great Britain in 1982 and 1986.

Peter followed the all-time greats, Keith Holman, Barry Muir, Billy Smith, Tommy Raudonikis and Steve Mortimer, and was equally as good as those players. I first saw Peter Sterling in an Australian coaching video. He was a very young player who was going through the skills and coaching drills for passing, handling, tackling, kicking and catching. He was easily recognisable with his flowing, long blonde hair, a trademark he kept throughout his career and, of course, the ease with which he carried out his duties on the video.

He was a natural footballer. Not big or powerful, Peter was short in height, athletically built, nippy, but not exceptionally fast. Holman was a stocky, nuggety player with great speed off the mark, Muir and Smith were fast, elusive runners and Raudonikis was a destroyer, a fighter who loved the hard, tough world of test matches and mixing it with the Pommie forwards. But Sterling was the Rolls Royce among the 4x4s, a master tactician, a planner and plotter. He would bring on the big forwards to get the opposition on the back foot, then bang, he would introduce a wide play that caught them out. He was a super scrum-half with the foresight of a modern player and the old-fashioned skills of yesteryear.

His half-back partners benefited from his expertise too. Brett Kenny, who played at both club and international level with him for years, always rated Peter as his best partner and Kenny himself was one of Australia's best players ever, either at stand-off or at centre.

Sterling burst into British rugby league like a breath of fresh air. His first tour, with the 'Invincibles', in 1982, showed just how far in front of Great Britain the Australians had raced. Even when in the positions at receiving the ball from a kick-off, we were still placing our half-backs to mark the short 10-yards kick from the centre spot. Sterling, instead, would stand deep, as he was a brilliant catcher of a high ball and would gain possession, pass to a big forward to run the ball at the opposition, then be set to take the pivot's role from the forward's play-the-ball. Everything was worked out to the last detail.

He and Kenny became legends in Australian test football and at the Parramatta club where both played from being youngsters to retirement. Peter's second love, after his national commitments, was New South

Wales, his state and, again along with Brett Kenny, he played many matches against Queensland. At this time, Peter's two biggest challengers for the number seven shirt were Steve Mortimer and Mark Murray. Mortimer was renowned for his cover defence and game-making skills. Murray, like Holman, was all aggression and power. Peter withstood their challenge before, in a short spell for Hull FC, he endeared himself to the Boulevard supporters.

The youthful Lee Crooks and Garry Schofield learned much as youngsters playing in the same side as Sterlo. The strange irony of Peter's one Wembley appearance for Hull FC was that in the game against Wigan in the 1985 Challenge Cup Final, Brett Kenny was in the Lancashire team's line-up. Wigan won a close encounter and Kenny, to rub it in, won the Lance Todd Trophy. Peter did win a prestigious man-of-the-match award when he picked up the White Rose trophy when Hull FC beat Hull KR in the 1984-85 Yorkshire Cup Final 29-12 and, in the same season, Hull KR reversed the result in the Regal Trophy Final, winning 12-0, with Peter receiving a runners up medal.

Peter played in four Grand Finals in Sydney, when Parramatta won the title in 1981, 1982, 1983 and 1986; a wonderful record.

He was coached by some of the finest in the Australian game, including Jack Gibson, John Monie, Frank Stanton and Don Furner. He gained 18 Australian test caps, 13 New South Wales jerseys and represented City in the prestigious City versus Country games.

A player who knew the game and the art of scrum-half play inside out, Peter went into media work on retiring from football and still does regular analysis on the weekly Australian games which come to us via Sky Television as well as writing weekly columns for several national newspapers in Australia.

My lasting memory of him was the sporting and generous way in which he took both victory and defeat. Although defeat did not come often, when it did he could handle it. A superb sportsman who made friends throughout the rugby league-playing world with his typical outgoing Australian nature and goodwill, Peter Sterling was born to be a hero and he became one.

	App	Tries	Goals	Pts
Parramatta	229	47	16	186
Hull FC	36+2	9	0	36
New South Wales	13	0	0	0
Australia	18	4	1	16

Mick Sullivan

I had heard a lot about Mick Sullivan, the flying wingman from Shaw Cross, from my Dad. He had heard about him from a workmate who lived in the little cross-road village on Leeds Road, at the very top of the Leeds 'cutting', very near the Shaw Cross pit in Dewsbury.

So, when I went to a big match at Odsal, I was pleased to see that one Michael Sullivan was playing for the Yorkshire under-18 side against Lancashire in a curtain raiser. Although he was from a younger age group, 'Sully' had a blinder and not long after he and his centre partner, a very good player named Wainwright, were signed by the then cream of Yorkshire rugby league, Huddersfield.

Sully made great strides and was in and out of the first team almost immediately. This period coincided with my signing for Hull FC in 1953. We won our way to the old reserve-team Yorkshire Senior Cup Final that year and faced the mighty Huddersfield 'A' team at Fartown. The game was played in the evening, in torrential rain, with Huddersfield the eventual winners. In their excellent side were Frank 'Spanky' Dyson, Wainwright, Bob Thompson and the great Mick Sullivan.

The following season, Sully was selected for the first ever Rugby League World Cup, played in France in 1954 and, on winning the World Cup, he became a hero overnight. He was a regular member of the national side from then until the 1963 season when, playing club rugby for York, he was selected for the final time to play against the Australian tourists. Sully won a record 46 caps for his country, and his pairing with Billy Boston became as well known as 'bread and dripping' in the north of England.

Sully was top try-scorer only once in all his years in the top flight when, playing for Wigan in 1957-58, he crossed for 50 tries. However, his defence must have saved many, many more than that because he was a hard, devastating tackler who left many an opponent wondering if he was on this earth or Fuller's. His clashes with Australian hard-man threequarter, Peter Diamond, are legend, particularly on the 1958 tour when he crossed for tries no fewer than 38 times.

Touring again in 1962 he scored 14 tries, but besides his try-scoring capabilities, Sully's value was in being the perfect tourist. If there was an injury in the back division, Sully would fill in. He played as a winger, centre, stand-off and even scrum-half in a test against New Zealand in 1962 in Auckland.

He was a tough man too and would stand no nonsense from anyone. He would be sent off while taking on bigger men in on-field tussles. In the third test in 1962, Sully 'walked' along with Derek Turner and in the big Lions versus New South Wales game, six men were dismissed, three from the Australians and Bill Sayer, Boston and Sullivan, as if to prove that you didn't mess with the tourists in those days, even the wingmen.

While one could wax lyrical about the tries Sully scored, the defensive part of his game was special. His tackles were not all made on the touchline either, many were made in covering role. One in particular is worth remembering. It was on a winter's afternoon at Headingley, in the first round of the Challenge Cup, Leeds versus Wigan in 1959, and a real tough cup-tie it was. Sully had joined Wigan from Huddersfield for a world record £9,500 in 1957-58. Leeds were in front 5-0, when Derek Hallas, Leeds's speedy centre, was put clear from the half-way line in the centre of the field. It would be another try to Leeds and the goalkick would give Leeds the edge with a 10-0 lead, or so thought the Leeds fans. Sully had other thoughts. Tearing across from the left wing, he gradually overhauled Hallas and with one final dive at the flying centre, brought him down heavily, inches short of the line.

Wigan went on to win the game 12-5, and the tackle by Sully must have gone a long way to securing victory. Wigan went on to beat Hunslet, Halifax and then Leigh 5-0, in a hard-fought semi-final and went on to Wembley to beat Hull FC 30-13, in a one-sided match. But what if Sully had missed Hallas? Who knows?

In January 1961, he moved from Wigan to St Helens, again for a world record fee, this time £11,000, staying there until 1963, when he moved to York.

His swansong came in 1966. Sully was playing at loose-forward and as player-coach, took Dewsbury to the Challenge Cup semi-final, only to be beaten by St Helens 12-5. Saints went on to beat Wigan 21-2 in the final.

Sully had a theory of why the touring Australians of 1982 and 1986 were so good and so unbeatable. "It's this way" he explained "we toured in 1958 and fathered 'em all". When retired as a footballer, Sully went into the prison service as a warder and served on the maximum security wing at Wakefield Prison. He says that he is glad that his defensive qualities were not needed there. One of the game's biggest and best heroes is Mick Sullivan, originally a plumber from Pudsey, near Leeds.

	App	Tries	Goals	Pts
Huddersfield	117	93	0	279
Wigan	125	84	0	252
St Helens	82	32	0	96
York	26	7	0	21
Dewsbury	40	2	0	6
Yorkshire	14	13	0	39
England	3	2	0	6
Great Britain	46	41	0	123

Ken Traill

Son of a professional rugby league player, Jim Traill, Ken also had a younger brother, Andy, who played for many years at Keighley. The family had a local public house in Hunslet, The Prospect, and there were always a few rugby league players in the pub.

Born in Northumberland, Ken learned his rugby league at the famous Hunslet Carr School and was the typical tall, lean, superb footballer that the district of Hunslet produced year-in, year-out.

Ken's ball-handling was a delight to behold. He could find a runner coming short onto him with the deftest of gentle passes that were impossible to drop, or he would split a defence with a 20-yard, arrow-straight pass that went like a bullet into the runner's hands. So classical was his passing that a photo of Ken, playing for Bradford Northern, and in full stride with hands and feet in the correct position and eyes transfixed on the target area and the ball drawn back in the ultra perfect pose, was on the main page entitled 'Passing and Handling' in a superb little booklet, that in my day no self-respecting player was without: the Leeds and Hunslet Schools coaching manual.

From this little blue-backed booklet, filled with the basic teachings of the best way to produce the many skills of the game, came the Morocco bound classics of today in describing the basics of our game. Ken was also a copybook tackler for such a tall man. Standing six feet two inches and weighing up to about 16 stones as he aged, Ken signed for his local side Hunslet and played in the first team regularly, but it was not long before Bradford Northern, stirring themselves after the six years of war and building on a Challenge Cup Final win over Leeds in the second competition after the war, signed the young fair-haired classical forward and whisked him away to Odsal.

Ken went to Wembley two years on the trot with Bradford, losing to Wigan in 1948 by 8-3, but beating Halifax 12-0 in 1949. Widnes stopped a fourth visit in four years when the Chemics beat Bradford 8-0 in the semi-final in 1950. But Ken found satisfaction when he was selected to tour with the Lions that year and although Harry Street, then of Dewsbury, played in all three tests against the Australians, Ken was at loose-forward in the two Kiwi tests to gain two of his eight international caps.

He was back on the 1954 tour with Dickie Williams as captain and Dave Valentine as his loose-forward partner. Ken played in one test each against the Australians and Kiwis.

In club football, Ken and Arthur Clues had many a battle-royal because the clashes between Leeds and Bradford were sometimes bloodbaths. Bad blood from the 1946 tour would burst to the fore in these league matches and I well remember an end-of-season game, played in brilliant sunlight at Headingley, during which Bradford Northern had Leeds to the sword. With Bradford winning by a fair margin, Ken and big Arthur had been at it all afternoon and only in the final seconds of the game did Arthur get the chance to show his brilliant best when be charged onto a pass and, using that superb step of his, smashed through two tacklers to plough under the posts for a consolation try. As he dived for the try, Ken joined in the four-man tackle; big Arthur secured the touchdown, but received a horrendous cut on the eyebrow which pumped out blood as though it was from a tap.

I was only a kid, but I was standing only a matter of three yards from the incident, and saw no foul play. However, Ken did say something to Arthur as he climbed to his feet and the remark caused one of the longest fights on a playing field that I ever witnessed. Arthur's blood was everywhere as he and Ken battled it out, joined by almost every player on the field. The referee blew his whistle for full time and players from both sides stopped fighting and pulled the two warriors apart.

Later, Ken had several seasons at Halifax, including one monumental third round Challenge Cup game at Thrum Hall in 1957, when he played number 13 for Halifax while Harry Street was at number 13 for Leeds, the two having toured together in 1950. Ken crossed for two tries that day, but Leeds won 16-10 and went on to beat Barrow at Wembley.

His next move was to Wakefield in 1957 and he took over as coach in 1958, staying there for 12 seasons and winning just about everything a coach could win. He actually won his final Yorkshire cap in 1959 as a Trinity player. Ken had been withdrawn from the Yorkshire team when it was found out that he was in fact a Northumbrian, but was allowed to play again after a change to the qualification rule.

He died in March 2002 after suffering from Alzheimer's disease and will be remembered as one of the all time great loose-forwards. The only time I played against the wonderful Ken Traill was when we were both blind-side props. His skills were legend, and so is this hero.

	App	Tries	Goals	Pts
Hunslet	50	2	0	6
Bradford Northern	315	37	3	117
Halifax	90	12	0	36
Wakefield Trinity	28	1	0	3
Yorkshire	11	1	0	3
England	4	1	0	3
Great Britain	8	1	0	3

Derek Turner

I begin this piece with trepidation. How can I describe the sheer determination of a born winner, a player who could inspire others with the same intensity as himself? He was the best pack leader I ever saw. He did not have the silky skills of Johnny Whiteley or the craftiness of Billy Iveson, but was very similar to Vince Karalius: all win, hard tackles and win again.

He was not the biggest loose-forward to ever play, in fact people reckon his best weight was around 13 to 14 stones, but at more than six feet tall, Derek was 100 per cent fit, strong and tough.

Derek learned his rugby league at junior level at the Cathedral Boys School, Wakefield, Balne Lane, Alverthorpe Boys Club in Ossett and that prolific producer of good players, Shaw Cross Boys Club in Dewsbury. At 18-years-old Derek signed for Hull Kingston Rovers and, after making his Yorkshire county debut in the second-row in 1954, he joined the Army to do his national service.

Playing rugby union in the forces to keep in perfect fitness, Derek emerged from the Army to be transferred for £2,750 to Oldham. At The Watersheddings, Derek tasted his first professional success and his cabinet was soon filling with winners' medals when, between 1956 and 1958, the strong Oldham side won the prestigious Lancashire Cup three times, the Lancashire League title twice and the League Championship. It was during this time at Oldham that the rip-roaring second-rower became one of the best loose-forwards in the league and Derek gained his first close look at the 'enemy', Australia, when he was selected to play in two games against them in 1956. His determination and desire to win earned him selection in the 1957 World Cup series played in Australia and New Zealand. He also continued to gain county selection.

In March 1959 Wakefield paid Oldham £8,000 as Derek Turner came home to Yorkshire. Not many people realised that both Trinity and Derek were on the verge of great things in the seasons to come. And this started in 1960 with a Wembley win against Hull FC and a Yorkshire Cup Final win over Huddersfield. In fact Derek lifted the Challenge Cup in 1960, 1962 and 1963, together with the Yorkshire Cup in 1961.

In his playing career Derek played 213 times for Wakefield, 140 for Hull KR and 134 for Oldham. He holds an almost unique record alongside only a few world-class players - in this country he won every available honour open to him, the Challenge Cup, Championship, Yorkshire Cup, Lancashire Cup, Yorkshire League, Lancashire League, County Championship with Yorkshire, 24 test caps for Great Britain including captaining the Lions tourists in New Zealand in 1962 and he also played for England against France in 1962-63.

What a record this is, and all this playing above his weight, gaining a reputation second-to-none and in the most exposed position on the field, loose-forward. In 1965, after a year in retirement, Derek came back to Trinity to help because the club was in the process of rebuilding and he played in 24 matches. He attempted to continue in 1966 but suffered a shoulder dislocation that finally took its toll and forced his full retirement.

Such a wonderful playing career with so much top experience could not finish there and Derek joined Castleford as head coach. He made an immediate impression and in 1968-69 he took his charges to both the Yorkshire Cup and Challenge Cup finals and the Championship final: three major finals in one season.

Leeds beat Castleford in both the Yorkshire Cup and Championship Finals, but Derek's team brought the Challenge Cup back to Castleford, beating Salford 11-6 at Wembley. The following season, 1970, Castleford were back at the twin towers again, this time beating Wigan 7-2.

In one of the biggest shocks for some time, Derek was appointed coach of Leeds for the 1970-71 season. His record at Headingley was excellent. A Wembley appearance in 1971 gave Derek a superb coaching CV, but a shock 24-7 defeat by Leigh was only eased a bit by a Yorkshire Cup win the same season. Yet again Derek saw his team win through to Wembley in 1972, giving him the supreme success of four Wembley finals on the trot, but again there was defeat, this time by St Helens. However, a great Championship win against the Saints eased the pain of that Wembley reverse. The impact of another Yorkshire Cup win at Odsal over Dewsbury in 1973 was wiped out when Dewsbury turned the tables on Leeds in the Championship Final with an historic win.

Despite his tremendous record, Derek was released from the Leeds coaching position and, although he did return to Wakefield as coach for a short spell in the 1980s, he could not repeat his former successes. So, 'what can one say about Derek Turner' has been answered as well as I can. He is a legend in our game, both as player and as coach, a hero in both departments.

	App	Tries	Goals	Pts
Hull KR	140	27	0	81
Oldham	134	35	1	107
Wakefield Trinity	213	45	0	135
Yorkshire	10	2	0	6
England	1	0	0	0
Great Britain	24	8	0	24

Dave Valentine

Not that long after the Second World War, the famous Huddersfield club travelled up to the border country to snare one of the best ever Scottish signings, David Valentine. Dave was snatched away from his home club, Hawick, the supplier of so many great rugby union players who came south and made the grade in the XIII-a-side game. Dave was ready-made for the position of loose-forward: tough, strong, quick for a big man and with that special bravery that seems to be bred north of the border.

Well over six feet and weighing a superbly proportioned 15 stones, Dave Valentine followed a well-trodden trail that exchanged the glorious countryside of southern Scotland, with its rural lifestyle, its salmon and trout rivers, rolling banks and braes, for the sooty factory chimney stacks, pit-heads and grimy streets of back-to-back houses in the industrial north of England.

Those marvellous areas around Hawick, Melrose, Kelso, Selkirk, Gala and Jedburgh produced many great rugby league players, including Alex Fiddes the classical centre who came to Huddersfield, international forward Willie Welsh to York, the flying wingman Drew Turnbull and his centre partner Tommy Wright at Leeds, the brothers Cowan - Stan to Hull FC and Ronnie to Leeds - and Drew Broach who served Leeds and Hunslet so well. Charlie Renilson went to Halifax and David Rose to Huddersfield along with the Powderhall sprinter Jock Anderson. George 'Happy' Wilson joined Workington Town and thrilled the Cumbrians with his speed, Whitehaven signed the brilliant Brian Shillinglaw the top scrum-half from Galashiels, and the Cumbrians later brought down between them, Alan Tait, Alex Cassie and Brian Lauder. The biggest purchase was when Wigan swooped for George Fairbairn from Kelso and there was a lesser one when Wakefield bought John Hegarty from Hawick. All these Scots ignored the signs so predominately situated in and around these border rugby union clubs, 'No rugby league men admitted', and thankfully so did Dave Valentine, who besides playing 15 times for Great Britain, was part of arguably the best back three in the game when he played for the Other Nationalities on many occasions, as part of the famous trio that also included Arthur Clues and Harry Bath.

Dave toured as a Lion, on the 1954 tour after making his international debut against the touring Australians in 1948. On returning from the 1954 tour, the selectors sat down to pick the 1954 World Cup squad to represent Great Britain in France. Originally selecting a side from the recent tour, the whole game in this country was astounded to hear that only three of the tourists were prepared to accept the selection, giving the official reason that the World Cup competition was too soon after the Australian tour. It seemed the Australians did not have that problem, as their team that competed in France was mostly that which had beaten Great Britain by two tests to one in the recent series.

Phil Jackson, Gerry Helme and Dave Valentine were the only three original tourists to accept the World Cup invitation, with Dave being asked to captain the side. So the door was open for a good few players to make their mark as future long-term internationals. The squad that did represent Great Britain covered themselves with glory as they went on to triumph against all the odds with a team of almost unknown heroes. Two youngsters in particular went on after this international debut to big things: Don Robinson with 10 caps and a brilliant career at Wakefield Trinity and Leeds with many selections for Yorkshire, and Mick Sullivan whose deeds on the international field are legend.

The fatherly lead given by Dave is written in the British game's history. He is still worshipped by the Huddersfield supporters who were lucky enough to see him play. Dave's power of personality and will-to-win were tremendous. Dave introduced brother Rob to Fartown and he too represented Great Britain against Australia in test football and went on to play successfully at Belle Vue for Wakefield Trinity. But Dave was a crucial figure in that wonderful Fartown side in the Cooper, Hunter, Devery era in the late 1940s and indeed skippered the claret and golds to Wembley victory in 1953. This final is remembered as 'Ramsden's match' when the young teenager Peter Ramsden on his birthday, scored both Huddersfield's tries, broke his nose and won the Lance Todd Trophy.

A fine player and a wonderful gentleman, Dave and his back-row partners, Clues and Bath were accepted as the best back three of their day and, on top of that, his captaincy of Great Britain, his World Cup success and his leadership of a team of no-hopers to that historic 1954 World Cup triumph is enough to classify him as an outstanding hero.

The title of the moving anthem, *Flower of Scotland* sums up this superb athlete, sadly no longer with us, who was one of the best.

	App	Tries	Goals	Pts
Huddersfield	318	62	0	186
Other Nationalities	16	3	0	9
Great Britain	15	2	0	6

Tom van Vollenhoven

There has always been something special about South African backs, especially wingmen, who change codes and play rugby league. I remember seeing this tall, blonde Afrikaner on the newsreels, running like a Springbok, scoring tries against the touring British rugby union boys and making it look easy.

The player opposite him in that rugby union Lions tour of 1955 was Tony O'Reilly of Ireland, who was a good rugby player but wished he had stayed in the Emerald Isle after 'The Van' had finished with him. Tom played in all five tests against the Lions, and then made the tour to Australia and New Zealand with the South African national team. In September 1957 St Helens paid the princely sum of £4,000 to bring the former Pretoria policeman to the heartland of Lancashire, and to his new football home, Knowsley Road.

The small group of sports writers who gathered that day to welcome this tall, blonde, bronzed athlete posed question after question and, true to Tom's ways, received simple answers, with no promises, except one. "Just show me the line, and I'll go for it" vowed the Springbok flyer. That statement, via the press, was reported by none other than the late, great, Eddie Waring who covered the arrival of The Van. So after the ballyhoo came the reckoning and the faith of the Saints board was there to see, as they threw this untried rooky rugby union wingman in against a strong Leeds side in a home league game.

Many more than 20,000 people packed into Knowsley Road to see what this top union flyer could do, and it was well worth waiting for as he gained possession almost on the half-way line and showed tremendous acceleration to clear the frantic Leeds cover, then left the poor Leeds full-back grasping at thin air as he flew over for a try to the delight of those knowledgeable Saints supporters.

Like most of the all-time great wingmen, he could tackle too. As a South African rugby player, The Van lost none of his natural aggression - that tough, decisive attitude to his rugby that was bred in the Afrikaner of his day. Jim Sullivan saw his first game and smacked his lips as he passed his vastly experienced opinion on this newcomer: "We have seen nothing yet from this lad. I think he will be a sensation." How prophetic.

His try-scoring feats rate with any in the history of our game, even the fabulous Albert Rosenfeld of Huddersfield, and this magnificent runner scored many wonder tries. Was there any better than his length of the field effort in the 1959 Championship final at Odsal against a very good Hunslet side in Saints 44-22 win?

There was also the classic try that all who witnessed the 1961 Challenge Cup Final at Wembley against the old enemy, Wigan, remember. That pulsating game was reaching a climax as The Van broke down the touchline. Challenged by his fellow countryman, Fred Griffiths, he passed inside to team mate Ken Large, who had a long way to go and with the valiant Eric Ashton chasing and gaining every stride. The try line was approaching, but could Large hold off the Wigan captain and reach the whitewash? No, Ashton had worked wonders to run down the flying Large and the chance was lost. But then, at the last second who came jetting along the sideline to take Large's desperate pass outside? It was The Van and, as Ashton nailed Large only inches short, Tom was putting the ball down for a magnificent try. He was a showstopper and a winner. Saints took the trophy 12-6.

My personal heartbreak moment relating to The Van came while playing for Dewsbury against St Helens at Crown Flatt in the late 1950s. Saints were riding high at the top of the league, full of internationals, while Dewsbury were the team of odds-and-ends. It seemed that all Saints had to do that December afternoon was turn up. But with only minutes to play, we were in front by four points and camped near the Saints line. A scrum five yards from the Saints try line and Saints hooker Bob Dagnall took one against the head, Austin Rhodes picked up the ball and fed Vince Karalius on the blindside and the great man took three determined tacklers to him before slipping the perfect one-handed pass to the wingman. All we had to do was make one last tackle and we had won. However, the wingman was the fabulous Van and he simply sped 80 yards to score, beating his opposite number and our full-back on the way. Rhodes landed the conversion and we lost by a point.

As consolation, something happened that day of which I had never seen before in a rugby league game, the Saints' players made two lines and applauded us off the field.

Tom van Vollenhoven topped the try charts for three years on the trot, in 1958-59, 1959-60 and 1960-61, with 62, 54 and 61 tries respectively. As Jim Sullivan said: "Tom van Vollenhoven was a sensation" and a hero.

	App	Tries	Goals	Pts
St Helens	409	392	0	1,176

Harold Wagstaff

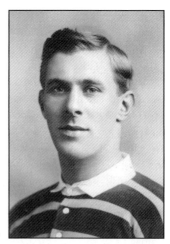

If H. H. 'Dally' Messenger was the Australian all-time great centre, then Harold Wagstaff was his Great Britain counterpart. First seen as a 15-year-old, playing in the Bradford and District League for Underbank Rangers, this boy was blessed to become, in the opinion of many good judges, the finest centre threequarter ever to pull on a boot. When folk spoke of him, they rarely mentioned his birth name, but more often referred to him by the nickname, 'The Prince of Centres'. In the wonderful book *The Roots of Rugby League*, author Trevor Delaney tells of Huddersfield's Mr John Clifford signing Harold Wagstaff for five gold sovereigns. Around the same time, 1906, Huddersfield also signed a very good player from Swansea, Jim Davies, a half-back who toured with the first British Lions in 1910. In comparison, the Welsh player demanded, and received, 140 gold sovereigns to come north.

Wagstaff made his debut for Huddersfield at the Barley Mow ground, Bramley, on 10 November 1906, still only 15 and he scored his first try for the claret and golds in the second half. The young prodigy caused a stir in the still-fledgling league because of his boyish looks, and, as a precaution, the Huddersfield club inserted a reproduction of his birth certificate in the match programme in the big crowd pulling game against Leeds at Fartown when The Prince made his home debut on 1 December 1906. We can see the vastly different attitude that the young Wagstaff had compared to the old stiff upper lip of the union game, when, at 17-years-old and interviewed before his first county trial, he said: " I have decided not to kick the ball. I will run with it. I am selected as a threequarter whose job is to run with the ball and make play for others who are prepared to run and handle the ball," and he did.

He represented England before his 18th birthday, but was considered too young to play opposite Dally Messenger on the first Lions tour of Australia in 1910, so the selectors went for the experience of Jim Lomas, Bryn Jenkins and Joe Riley. At this time, Huddersfield were building up a side that would write its name in the history books of rugby league and because of its outstanding, crowd-pleasing displays of fast, open, running rugby, it became known as the 'Team of all the Talents'.

Wagstaff was the captain of the team and also captain of the second Lions tour in that horrendous year of 1914. The tourists returned home to a country at war with Germany, after an historic and victorious tour in which the famous 'Rorke's Drift' test was played. Forced by the Australians to play a third test in eight days and with a long injury list, the

Lions were down to 10 men as further injuries took their toll, but responding to a pre-match cablegram from the Northern Union in Leeds, which read: "England expects every man to do his duty", they did just that, winning the test 14-6.

Wagstaff's club mate at Fartown, Stanley Moorhouse, was the leading try-scorer on tour with 19 tries and The Prince scored 11 in 13 games. Most of the international side joined up on returning home and many were placed in the Army Service Corps. Harold was joined by two of his Huddersfield team-mates, Ben Gronow the big Welsh rugby union international, and his mate from the 1914 tour, Dougie Clark, the Cumberland champion wrestler.

The Army Service Corps was full of the top Northern Union men, who played what is now rugby league, and wowed southern rugby union supporters with their fast running game, with very little kicking.

The horrific war ended in 1918 and tours to Australia resumed in 1920. Now almost 30 years of age, Harold captained the Lions for a second time but on this occasion Great Britain lost the Ashes. The Prince could look back on a glittering career though, many cups and medals won, two Lions tours as captain and those glorious years as captain of the 'Team of all the Talents' who performed wonders, year after year, to make the claret and gold jersey respected to this day.

Albert Rosenfeld scored his fantastic 80 tries in a season for Huddersfield in 1913-14, just another fact to prove the quality of that great side.

Harold Wagstaff remains a legend, years after his demise in 1939 aged 48. A friend of mine went to Harold's funeral, and insists the following story is true. As his coffin was carried along the path to his grave, a series of gas lamps lit the way in the evening gloom. As the coffin passed each gas lamp, my friend honestly believes, they dimmed, in a final mark of respect for the world's best centre threequarter.

He must have been a most electrifying player, a thinker years ahead of his time and a much-liked man because he could inspire his team mates to great heights, even when they thought they could go no further. Harold Wagstaff was the stuff heroes are made of.

	App	Tries	Goals	Pts
Huddersfield	436	175	12	549
Yorkshire	15	4	0	12
Great Britain	12	2	0	6
England	9	7	3	27

David Ward

David played, and was involved in, rugby
league since a young schoolboy at St Austin's
Catholic School in Wakefield. He made the
school team as a rip-roaring loose-forward
and, a tribute to him in the excellent little
book *Wakefield's Sporting Catholics*, tells of
the superb Wakefield, Huddersfield, St Helens
and Great Britain forward, Brian Briggs,
coaching the juniors, including David, on the
school field near the gasworks.

David moved through the local rugby
league system and ended his junior career at
the prolific producer of top rugby league players, Shaw Cross Boys Club at
Dewsbury. From Shaw Cross, which gave Great Britain three international
hookers in the decade between 1972 and 1982, in Mick Stephenson,
David Ward and John Dalgreen, David signed as a professional for Leeds
in May 1971.

He talks with pride of playing six times for his county of origin,
Yorkshire, four of those appearances as captain, and he also captained
Great Britain against France at The Boulevard, Hull in 1981. This ranks
highly in David's list of successes in the game, together with the other 11
times he was capped by his country. His collection of winners' medals,
and only a few runners'-up ones, is very impressive and his two Wembley
Challenge Cup Final wins as captain in 1977 and 1978 were achieved
when at his peak as both captain and player.

David was one of the last of the old-time hookers. The guys who
nestled in the centre of the scrum, that cauldron of physical pain and
strain and, in those days, downright violence, had to be of iron-hard
character and of a toughness not required today with the changes in the
operation of scrums. To have to be able to look after one's self is a vast
understatement of what was required. A hooker then had to be a
combination of a skilled rugby league player, all-in wrestler and
professional pugilist. David filled all three roles to the full and was a much
respected opponent too.

I first saw David as a Leeds player when I joined Dewsbury's coaching
staff in 1972 and he was just breaking into the first team. His leadership
qualities were always obvious and his general toughness was apparent as
his game, because it had to be then, was built on pure aggression. As a
club coach, my first time coaching against David, was in the Challenge
Cup first round at Headingley, when David led his team to a 25-5 victory
over my Halifax side in 1978. It was my first match in charge as senior
coach and at a new club. How I wished for a player of David's ability,
never thinking of what may happen some six years later. He bossed the

play around the field and the final margin of that victory was actually a confidence booster to my lads because we, at Halifax, were transfixed at the bottom of the Second Division and the fabulous Leeds were riding high in the First. Two seasons later, I took my Halifax team to the Final of the Yorkshire Cup and played Leeds, again at Headingley (the final venue had been decided before the competition started) and although still in the Second Division, we had improved and kept Leeds much nearer as they won the Cup 15-6. I maintain it would have been much closer had not my captain, playmaker and grand leader, Mick Blacker, been carried off after a tough tackle by David Ward.

It was all in the game in those days. In October 1983 my wish came true when I was appointed coach of Leeds and I inherited David as captain, which I considered an honour. Under his outstanding leadership on the field we won the John Player Trophy and also began a club-record equalling run of 18 games unbeaten. Later, as Great Britain coach, I discussed with David privately which hooker should play in the national side. He recommended David Watkinson of Hull Kingston Rovers and I accepted his sound advice.

David's love of the game and his obvious talents in communication, naturally led him into coaching at Hunslet and his first success was to gain promotion into the First Division in 1986-87, but without the vital finances they went down again the following season. I had moved to Cumbria, to Workington Town, and David was out of the game. I decided he had enough left to do a great job for me, on the field, with the youngsters up at Derwent Park. He agreed to join me and we had some good times on the long drive, twice a week, up to the mountainous county.

One of the most enthusiastic players I have ever had the pleasure of working with and a man who is as straight as a die, David collected the Challenge Cup twice at Wembley, the Yorkshire Cup several times, the John Player Trophy twice and the Cumbrian Cup once. This victory was special, as the Cup was thrown to David after the match, in a petulant presentation ceremony. He caught it, said 'Thank you', and behaved like the champion he is, a hero.

	App	Tries	Goals	Pts
Leeds	442+20	40	17	143
Workington Town	9+1	0	0	0
Yorkshire	6	2	0	6
England	6	0	0	0
Great Britain	12	0	0	0

Ernest Ward

We in rugby league can feel proud that almost to a man our superstars of past and present are decent blokes who, in the main, are approachable and act as gentlemen when in company. Of course it is reasonable to assume that some are more gentlemanly than others, and in the late Ernest Ward we had a gentleman supreme. When you met him, even when he was an elder statesman of the game, one could feel his

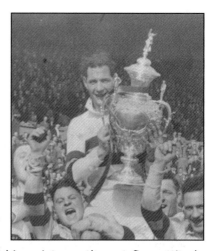

leadership qualities shine through and his quiet, gentle, yet firm attitude marked him out as one of life's leaders. In the age of part-time players, the average physique of all players in different positions was much smaller than that of today, but Ernest Ward possessed a superb build for a centre.

More than six feet tall and of athletic shape, Ernest was a master at every skill. A long strider with a great swerve, he practised the art of centre play by which he created space for his wing partner while his passing service to his wingman was perfect in timing and application. In club football, Ernest spent most of his playing time behind a pack of forwards that was going forward and allied to that he had the peerless Willie Davies as his stand-off half, who would make half openings for Ernest and his co-centre, Jack Kitching, in the wink of an eye. But Ernest Ward was not lifted to stardom by Willie Davies alone, he achieved that accolade by himself and by his own ability. Willie Davies, great player that he was, was just the icing on the Ward cake.

Born in Dewsbury, Ernest Ward captained every team he played for and was without doubt one of the best middle backs of his era. A reliable and long range goalkicker, his leadership of the Bradford Northern sides of the late 1940s through to the early 1950s and the Great Britain, England and Yorkshire teams of the same era shows what a good player he was because the national team at that time was very successful. This was achieved using his gentle, persuasive manner in the background, but leading from the front on the field. Ernest gained 20 caps for Great Britain and was a Lions tourist in 1946 and 1950, captaining the 1950 tour. After his playing career was over, Ernest took on the coaching mantle at several clubs before fully retiring from the game. His 12 tries and 95 goals on two tours shows his scoring ability, but it is when one looks at the number of tries his wingmen registered on tour, in the league and in various international matches that Ernest Ward's true strengths stand out.

Ernest's brother, Donald, was a great scrum-half in his own right and the pair figured superbly in Bradford Northern's tremendous post-war successes. A great gentleman as well as a great player, Ernest was always available with sound and experienced advice should anyone seek it, and his encouragement to young players with sensible suggestions to benefit their game is well known. But it is as a player, working his magic on the pitch and creating openings for his partners that Ernest is best remembered. On the 1946 tour, the game against Mackay District resulted Ernest creating a record which still stands. In a 94-0 drubbing, Ernest, playing at full-back, kicked 17 goals for a total of 34 points and this remains the record number of goals kicked and the highest individual points scored by any player in a match for Great Britain. He then captained Bradford Northern to three Wembley cup finals in three consecutive years, an 8-4 win in 1947 against Leeds, an 8-3 defeat in 1948 against Wigan, and a 12-0 victory in 1949 against Halifax.

My memory of Ernest Ward will always be of his display in the 1949-50 Yorkshire Cup Final at Headingley. He had an outstanding game in Bradford Northern's 11-4 victory over the star-studded Huddersfield side who featured the fabulous Lionel Cooper, Pat Devery and Johnny Hunter - three terrific Australian players. Ernest led his Northern side to a fine win despite being slight underdogs, before a massive 36,000 crowd. Two items of his play stand out for me. Under extreme pressure Ernest took a Willie Davies pass from a scrum only 10 yards from his own line and with a dummy, swerve and a little side step, ran the ball in a 60-yard curving run to set up an attack that brought a try to Northern. Later in the game, again under heavy pressure, Ernest saved a certain try when he took a flying Pat Devery into touch at the corner flag with the perfect covering leg tackle.

He was a tremendous player and a credit to our game, a true and superb ambassador to a sport he loved and a sport he served admirably throughout his long and ultra-distinguished career. Meeting him in his later years this gentleman still had the glint of steel in his eye but still maintained his touch with a 'velvet' glove. Ernest Ward - gentleman, sportsman and hero.

	App	Tries	Goals	Pts
Bradford Northern	391	117	538	1,427
Castleford	78	9	154	335
Batley	5	2	0	6
Yorkshire	10	6	6	30
England	20	2	26	58
Great Britain	20	4	22	56

Cliff Watson

By answering an advert in the *Sporting Chronicle* for players to play trials at St Helens, one of the game's hardest and best prop forwards held up his hand, left the Midlands and became a legend. A Londoner by birth, this rugby union second-row forward had represented the Hereford and Worcestershire combined counties team in the rugby union inter-county championship, and played for Dudley Kingswingford RUFC.

His second rugby league Challenge Cup tie after signing was the 1961 Final against St Helens's old enemy, Wigan. This game was won by Saints 12-6 and although the great Dick Huddart won the Lance Todd Trophy for the best player in the final, many good judges suggested that the new forward from rugby union could well have won it instead. The man was, of course, Cliff Watson.

Cliff went on to win 30 caps for Great Britain and make two Lions tours, in 1966 and the successful 1970 trip. But it was a far cry from success when he first donned the red, white and blue. The venue was Swinton, the year was 1963 and the opposition was the touring Australian Kangaroos. The result went into the record books as the biggest loss at that time for Great Britain when the Australians won 50-12.

Cliff's medal cabinet holds a goodly amount of winning gold with two Challenge Cup winners' medals in 1961 and 1966, both over the arch enemy Wigan, many Lancashire Cup winners as Saints won the cup on eight occasions from 1960-61 to 1968-69, coinciding with the years Cliff played at Knowsley Road. Cliff played in six of the eight wins. His tremendous value as a tourist is shown by him taking part in all 11 tests played on his two tours, six against the Australians and five against the Kiwis.

The front-row in the days of competitive scrummaging was a red-hot place for the hard stuff, particularly in test football. Unlike today, there was no 20 minutes on, 20 minutes off for front-rowers - it was the full 80 minutes, non-stop. This adds credence to the reputation Cliff Watson gained for being a top, go-forward player who would not take a backward step. The players that the Australians threw at him read like a "Who's Who" of the hardest men in Australia since Ned Kelly. In 1966 the tough New South Welshman Lloyd Weir came and went in one test only, then the hard Queenslander, John Wittenberg for the last two tests. The Kiwis too had a couple of big tough men in the giant Maori, Sam Edwards, and Robin Orchard to confront Cliff.

Four years later the hard tackling Jim Morgan from Sydney was set against the fearless Watson. In test number two it was a man with a big reputation as a hit man, Johnny Sattler who fronted our hero, and he went too, finally their trump card in the final test was Arthur Beetson, a battle which would have been worth seeing. But none could dampen the fire of Cliff Watson, he saw them all off. Then it was over to New Zealand and the Kiwis' tough prop Orchard again showed true courage by standing against Cliff in two tests, and when Cliff moved over to number eight in the final test he matched it with another tough Kiwi, Doug Gailey.

The 1970 World Cup in England followed the Lions tour and the unusual thing was that Great Britain lost only one game in the whole tournament, but that defeat was in the final at Headingley against Australia after the Australians had been beaten twice in the competition. Cliff's Australian opposition in that World Cup was big Bob O'Reilly and a battle royal it was. Cliff played in one further test match, against France at St Helens in March 1971, and his side recorded a 24-2 victory.

Not too long after that Cliff upped sticks and departed to Australia to play for the Cronulla Sharks. He continued where he left off and was responsible for a surge of success at the Australian club when in 1973 Cronulla reached the Grand Final for the first time but went down to the classy Manly side 10-7.

Cliff never returned to Britain to play, but the deeds he achieved here as a player makes one wonder how would he have figured in today's game? His physical attributes would fit perfectly into the needs of the modern game: he was big, strong, fit and fearless. He would cart the ball up all day, and his defensive qualities were faultless. His opponents will tell you that he was the outstanding blindside prop of his era, a workhorse, and a never-say-die winner. What more would be needed?

Cliff Watson was a star in the star-studded squad of his time as a Great Britain regular. The awesome front-row: Dennis Hartley, Tony Fisher and Cliff Watson struck fear into any side they faced and backed up the old philosophy that winning test matches starts in the front-row.

Would Cliff Watson's style fit into today's more professional profile? Well, if being able to play, and being trusted to give everything to the team means anything today then he would, but it can only be conjecture. He was, and is, a life long hero.

	App	Tries	Goals	Pts
St Helens	367+6	57	0	171
Cronulla	39	9	0	27
Great Britain	29+1	5	0	15

Les White

As a young kid discussing with other young kids the rights and wrongs of rugby league in our area, the only players we knew at York were Les White and Charlie Taylor. Charlie stayed at York for most of his career, but Les climbed up the ladder to international football and the top in club level with a move to the glitzy Wigan.

We all knew as kids that Leeds had let Jeff Moores, the great Australian centre, go to York but that was years ago and if Leeds were playing York at Headingley, the two to look out for was the second-rower White and the centre Taylor, the latter being recognisable because he was prematurely bald.

My Dad was a great fan of Les White: "A good honest grafter who can run and handle the ball well," he pontificated as we talked rugby on those cold winter evenings just after his demob from the army. Well Dad, and I'm sure you're listening to me up there, Les White developed into a lot more than a grafter who could run and handle a bit.

Les was the outstanding York forward immediately after the Second World War, to the extent of being in the selectors' eyes when the 1946 touring team was named. He became a Lion as a member of that tour and indeed formed a first-choice second-row combination along with Doug Phillips that played in all three tests against Australia and - with Trevor Foster - in the one test against New Zealand. Les played in 18 of the 27 games on tour and scored six tries.

His tremendous cover tackling and willingness to accept the hard grafting required in those days cemented his place in the test side and didn't go unnoticed at home because, when he arrived back from the tour, he almost immediately agreed to be transferred across the Pennines to the fabulous Wigan club.

Les developed even further on joining the superb Lancashire champions and was recognised as a classy, quick-thinking forward who made a winning Wembley appearance in the cherry and white jersey in 1948 in the 8-3 win against Bradford Northern. Les had two further Great Britain appearances while at Wigan, against the touring Kiwis in 1947 giving him six caps in total plus several for his county, Yorkshire.

Although Wigan had paid a substantial fee to sign Les from York, the season after they signed the tough tackling Yorkshireman, Bill Hudson from Batley for a then record £2,000.

Because the war lasted six years, it played havoc with the careers of some players. Les was a casualty of this problem. Wigan agreed to transfer Les to Halifax and as soon as Bill Hudson settled in at Wigan, they let him return to his native county in 1949. He played only four seasons for the Thrum Hallers before an injury ended a war-interrupted career that would, according to many good judges, have produced one of Britain's best ever forwards but for the wartime break in his career. Halifax had the foresight to cover their investment with a good insurance policy and managed to recoup the majority of their outlay when Les was forced to retire. He was a potentially great forward who, because of his intelligent approach to his game, may well have been ahead of his time.

I must return to my dear old Dad and his analysis of Les. The old man knew of Les from before the war and had always rated him highly, and was surprised that one of the bigger clubs had not signed him as he thought that Les had great potential. Well Dad, you were correct. He developed to be good enough to play six times for Great Britain in the second-row when there were some good 'uns about, toured and was a success and was transferred to Wigan. I bow to your overall judgment.

And I do have a lingering memory regarding Les White. I saw him 'banjo' my childhood hero Arthur Clues at Headingley in a Leeds versus Wigan clash. Big Arthur took some knocking over, but Les did it with a beauty, right on the chin. I suppose it was a left-over from the 1946 tour as Arthur had played in all three tests against the tourists and maybe Les was straightening out the account. Come to think about it, as we are talking about heroes, Les must have been some hero to take on big Arthur. But he was, in my dear old Dad's eyes - so if he was good enough for Danny Bamford, he is a good enough hero for me.

	App	Tries	Goals	Pts
York	144	32	1	98
Wigan	69	26	0	78
Halifax	120	30	0	90
Yorkshire	7	0	0	0
England	11	4	0	12
Great Britain	6	0	0	0

John Whiteley

'Gentleman' John Whiteley, had the prefix given to him because of his 'true blue' demeanour both on the field and off it. He is a man who hardly ever changes no matter when you meet him, always greets you with a smile and a genuine word - a toff of a bloke and a toff of a forward. Wonderfully built for a loose-forward, John's physique was also ideal for the second-row, standing well over six feet and around 15 stones. His long stride when running clear devoured the ground, and he was therefore renowned for his speed and evasive qualities.

As a young player signing for Hull FC, I used to look in awe at the likes of Harry Markham, Bob Coverdale, Mick Scott, John Whiteley, Tommy Harris, Norman Hockley and the other fringe first team players and it was always John who spoke and made you feel at home. The Hull pack of forwards was among the strongest in the league around the early 1950s and their nemesis, the Halifax pack, had plenty of battles with them both at The Boulevard and at Thrum Hall. Among the Hull pack mentioned above and later added to with the inclusion of Cyril Sykes and Bill and Jim Drake, John Whiteley shone, even among these world class players and it was obvious that he was destined to be an international back-rower.

However, it was a hard road because in his era there were a large number of world class loose-forwards in this country, yet his talent and all round ability saw John join the ranks of Valentine, Traill, Karalius, Turner and Iveson. His first Great Britain cap was gained in the 1957 World Cup series in Australia and New Zealand when the other British loose-forward was the great Derek Turner. John became a full Lion on tour when he was selected for the 1958 trip down under with the courageous Alan Prescott as captain. Beaten in the first test with John at number 13, the second test was won in Brisbane in the historical game in which Alan Prescott played almost the whole match with a severely broken arm, and the back three that day was Dick Huddart, John Whiteley and Vince Karalius. What a back row, as impressive perhaps as the front row of Alan Prescott, Tommy Harris and Brian McTigue. Wow!

On that tour John played in four of the five tests, three of them in the second row. The one he missed was the final test in Auckland against the Kiwis. In all John played in 15 tests for Great Britain and allied to 12 appearances for Yorkshire and his one-club playing relationship at The Boulevard, it speaks volumes for his loyalty and big hearted play.

His deeds in the black and white irregular hoops of his beloved Hull FC's jersey are legend. And one particular performance in the red, white and blue of his country put John Whiteley into the folklore history of our game. It occurred on 21 November 1959 at Headingley and his actions had a double significance in its end result. Great Britain had, at that time, never lost a rugby league test match on the Leeds ground, but there, on that winter's afternoon, with the gloom approaching fast and a hint of snow in the air, Great Britain were facing not only defeat at Headingley, but an Ashes loss too, because the first test had seen a 22-14 Australian victory at Swinton. Now, with only minutes left on the clock, Great Britain were in danger of losing their proud unbeaten Headingley record. Gaining scrum five yards from the Australian line and some 20 yards from the posts, Jeff Stevenson, the former Leeds, now York half-back and Great Britain captain, seized the ball and shot away diagonally towards the Australian try line. The Ashes were at stake, and the whole Australian back-row swept away from the scrum to cover the quicksilver Stevenson. 'Make this tackle and we've won the Ashes' ran the Australians' thinking as their 11, 12 and 13 converged on the small, slim figure of the British scrum-half. Just at the point of no return, Stevenson's superb reverse pass, a back flip, found the ever-supporting Whiteley, as the Australians say, 'Following like a drover's dog', who accepted the pinpoint pass to drive over for the test match, and as it transpired Ashes winner, because the British team won the final test with an 18-12 win at Wigan. The Stevenson-Whiteley set planned move which won the game was practiced by every schoolboy half-back for years after.

My hero John Whiteley became the Hull FC and later, Hull KR coach and also coached Britain's last successful Lions tour in 1970 when John took out a superb side and confounded the world's critics by bringing home the Ashes. His coaching career encompassed the Yorkshire county side as well as the international squad and, just as he had been as a player, he was a very popular and excellent coach. To have seen this tall, well built, very quick, skilful attacking and defensive forward in his heyday gave immeasurable pleasure, a true hero.

	App	Tries	Goals	Pts
Hull FC	417	156	2	472
Yorkshire	12	4	0	12
England	1	0	0	0
Great Britain	15	2	0	6

Jack Wilkinson

Jack Wilkinson had the typical build for a front-rower, more than six feet tall, barrel-chested, immensely powerful and, at around 18 stones, a very big man indeed. A forward who never took a backward step, Jack took on all the top, tough props of his day, from all over the world, and was never bettered.

His rugby league career started in his Halifax school team and he had two junior clubs in Halifax Supporters under-16s and, up the hill from the town to the famous Siddal amateur side, again at under-16s. As a measure of his toughness, Jack had played in both under-18s and open-age football before he was 16 years old.

Always a big, strong player he was asked to play a trial game at the old Parkside ground for Hunslet in early 1947 and in those days Jack played either at loose-forward or in the second-row. He did not sign for Hunslet, but at the end of that season, after playing two trial games at loose-forward for Halifax, signed instead at Thrum Hall, making his first-team debut in the 1948-49 season against Warrington. Jack quickly made his strength pay and became a regular first-teamer soon after, and he became a cornerstone of the fabulous Halifax side of the early 1950s. The power of the Halifax pack was awesome and, selecting six from Mick Condon, John Thorley, Alvin Ackerley, Jack Wilkinson, Bryn Hopkins, Les Pearce, Derrick Schofield, Albert Fearnley and Des Clarkson gave the team plenty of options.

Season 1953-54 was a good one for Jack because he not only played in the famous drawn Challenge Cup Final against Warrington, 4-4 at Wembley, but in the replay too when an official crowd of 102,569, including myself, turned up at Odsal to see an 8-4 Warrington victory.

Jack also gained his first Great Britain cap against Australia in 1954 on tour and he was back at Wembley again with Halifax in 1956 but they lost to an excellent St Helens side 13-2.

Halifax and Hull FC were arch enemies at that time. The Hull pack was as powerful as the Halifax six and many bitter battles took place, especially in cup ties between the two clubs. The Yorkshire Cup Final in 1955 was a bloodbath with full scale fights breaking out all over the field. The game ended in a draw, 10-10, and the replay at Odsal saw Halifax successful 7-0. One reason behind the unruliness of this final was that in the previous year, 1954, the same two sides had also fought out the Yorkshire Cup Final, with Halifax winning a bad-tempered match 22-14.

At this time Jack was a regular in the Yorkshire County side and won several caps while a Halifax player. But it looked as though Wilkinson's county and international career was over when he was offered a lifeline to his career after Wakefield Trinity agreed a transfer fee with Halifax to take Jack to Belle Vue.

He made his Trinity debut at Wigan, and he played at Central Park just one week after helping Halifax to beat Trinity in the Yorkshire Cup at Thrum Hall in 1959. Wakefield paid the substantial sum of £4,500 for him and quite a few Trinity supporters lifted their eyebrows at such a high fee for a veteran. But Jack repaid every penny with five top seasons in which he regained his county and international place and cemented another selection on the successful 1962 tour, eight years after his first trip.

Three Challenge Cup wins, a Yorkshire Cup win, seven further Great Britain caps (giving Jack 13 in all), World Cup selection in 1960, two Yorkshire League winners' medals and two League Championship runners up medals followed. Jack played 151 games for Trinity and his farewell game was against Hunslet in February 1964.

In a career spanning 16 seasons, he played for England against Other Nationalities in 1953 and in 1960 he played for the Rest of the League in a World Cup trial, and gained World Cup selection on the strength of this game. Jack also played for a Rugby League XIII against France in 1956. He played against every test playing nation and at one time, for a short period, held the record of five Wembley appearances. He represented his county in the Lancashire and Cumberland games, and against Australian and New Zealand touring teams.

There have been many top prop forwards who have become legends in our game, but Jack Wilkinson must rate as one of the most successful. Leaving Wakefield, who released him for tremendous services rendered, Jack moved to the newly reformed Bradford Northern in 1964, as player-coach and he saw them regain their credibility in the Rugby Football League before retiring from the game to run a public house in Halifax. Jack passed away and is missed by a myriad of people from every aspect of the game he graced. A character, a good 'un and a hero.

	App	Tries	Goals	Pts
Halifax	252	22	0	66
Wakefield Trinity	151	10	0	30
Bradford Northern	11+1	0	0	0
Yorkshire	10	0	0	0
Great Britain	13	4	0	12
England	2	0	0	0

Dickie Williams

The stand-off that I 'grew up' with; he was the man who was the linchpin of the Leeds backs when I was a youngster learning rugby league by studying the game's better players. The ginger-haired Welshman was one of the outstanding stand-off halves of his day, having tremendous battles of skills with such as Willie Davies, Willie Horne, Ray Price, Ces Mountford, Russ Pepperell, Pat Devery, Arthur Talbot and many more.

Dickie settled into a Leeds team that boasted no fewer than eight Welshmen in the side, and continued a tradition of great players coming to the club from South Wales. Short in height and slight of build he was the archetypal Welsh stand-off, fleet of foot, quick into a gap, a terrific pair of hands, very brave in the tackle, excellent provider of openings for his centres, a superb supporter of forward breaks and an unselfish maker as well as scorer of wonderful tries.

The opposition players mentioned above were all in the same class as Dickie, and this again showed British club strength at stand-off. On reflection, and I watched this superb little player over quite a few years, I cannot recall him being an extraordinarily good kicker of the ball, in fact I can't remember having seen him ever kick it. That is why, possibly, he was such a brilliant rugby league stand-off, because he ran with the ball. He made openings for whoever was playing centre, not by kicking the ball away, but by running and deft handling. In those days of unlimited possession, the kicking game was one of many tactical ploys, unlike today's limited tackle game when it is sacrilege to be tackled on the last tackle and cough up a free set of six plays. In the past one did not kick as much in general field play because that would give away vital possession and it was harder to get the ball back then, but still, coming from rugby union, it was strange that Dickie did not kick more.

The other stand-offs mentioned above, apart from the excellent Willie Horne who could both kick and run the ball, were mostly runners and play-makers and Dickie Williams was one of the best. I recall several of the tries he scored as I watched him all those many years ago and, although time lends enchantment, they stay with me as though it were yesterday.

Hull played Leeds in the 1945-46 season and had played really well at Headingley to be leading the home side by three points in a mud bath of a game, with the dark of winter drawing in and the match into injury time, it looked as though Hull had gained a memorable victory at Leeds's expense. In the last play of the game, one tackle would have ended the match, but Williams gained possession playing towards the end of the ground that now houses the electric scoreboard, to the right of the posts running towards the North Stand. A step off his right foot saw him accelerate diagonally back towards the top South Stand corner flag to sell a superb dummy and straighten up to step off his left foot. He ran inside the full-back in thick, clinging mud and dived triumphantly over to avoid a defeat for his team. That the goalkick failed is of no consequence, the point was the wonderful try.

Another of the many crucial tries he scored was at Fartown in the semi-final of the Challenge Cup against Wakefield Trinity in 1947. I was at the game and was sitting on the grass surrounding the pitch in line with the try line over which he dived to register a super solo effort in the 21-0 win that sent the Loiners to Wembley. Earlier in that outstanding cup run Leeds had drawn the very dangerous and local old enemy, Hunslet, in the second round at Headingley. On a quagmire of a pitch, the game ebbed and flowed one way then the other, forwards dominating the play in a typically hard, tough cup tie. At 0-0, Chris Brereton trundled into a gap, passed to the supporting Arthur Clues and the Australian star looked to his right to find Dickie steaming up to take the big man's pass and run over the line for the only try of the tie. Bert Cook's goal gave Leeds a very hard-earned 5-0 win.

Dickie toured Australia and New Zealand as a Lion twice, in 1950 as a Leeds player and captained the 1954 tour as a Hunslet player. Considering the quality of stand-offs around in his time, his 12 Great Britain caps are testament to his ability, but on Dickie's tour as captain, an event occurred that had not happened before, or, since. A game between the tourists and New South Wales, in front of 30,000 spectators, was abandoned after fighting and all 26 players were ordered from the field by the referee, Aubrey Oxford. But even that can not detract from the reputation of the little ginger-haired Welsh wonder, another hero, Dickie Williams.

	App	Tries	Goals	Pts
Leeds	237	69	0	207
Hunslet	44	5	0	15
Great Britain	12	5	0	15
Wales	13	5	0	15

John Wolford

Signing for Bramley from the Balne Lane junior club, Wakefield, as a 16- year-old, John was another of those small youngsters of whom it was said: "He will never make it, he's too small". Well, John buckled down to the task while giving away stones in weight to his opponents and building up a technique that would help him survive in the tough world of professional rugby league as it was in those days. Very light - he weighed only eight stones when he signed - John had played either scrum-half or stand-off in junior football, but the coaching staff at McLaren Field put him at number seven from the start and John blossomed in that role. Just occasionally though, John was asked to play at stand-off and the coach would still get 100 per cent from him, no matter where he played. The promise of a good player was always around John, it shone like a halo, the Bramley supporters could see it each week. And he started to get bigger, slowly seeming to grow each week and began developing the strength that people thought he never would. An overriding memory I have of John, from when I used to watch Bramley on the occasional week off from playing, was of him running into a packed defence, and bursting through the ruck of defenders. He developed tremendous strength in his upper body and allied to his thickening physique, he became very hard to knock over.

Being a good handling footballer from his junior days, playing at this higher level honed this aspect of his play and his timing of passes was first class. John's determination was rewarded in 1970 when he was a surprise selection for the Yorkshire side to play Cumberland at Whitehaven. He played at stand-off half and, unfortunately for him, Yorkshire lost 21-15.

Although John maintained good club form he was never selected again for the county side. Bramley was still a low profile club with little or no chance to win anything and it was a struggle. John, along with his old mate Jack Austin, were the only two with the ability to move on from the club. Then, out of the blue, after John had already spent years at the club, Arthur Keegan arrived as assistant coach and a short time later took over from Keith Holliday as head coach. Things began to happen and Arthur brought a few new players to the club.

Suddenly the side took on a stronger appearance as the mid-season BBC Floodlit Trophy competition started in controversy. It was the 1973-74 season and the three-day-week imposed by the government, because of power cuts caused by the miners' strike, began to bite. Consequently, floodlights were not available so the Floodlit Trophy was played in the afternoon, in daylight. Bramley did remarkably well and fought their way to the final to take on the cup kings of Widnes at Naughton Park, and beat them on their own ground to register the first cup to be won by the club. Sadly, not long after, Arthur left the club and Peter Fox swept in to win promotion in his first season, but resigned to join the much bigger club, Bradford Northern in 1977.

Peter swooped to sign Derek Parker, Jack Austin and John from his old club Bramley, and take them into a new dimension of club success at Odsal. After four seasons, John moved on again, once more with Jack Austin, this time to Dewsbury and along with the great Bob Haigh formed a deadly trio in the Second Division.

It was while playing for Dewsbury in the 1979-80 season that they came to Halifax to play against my Thrum Hall side in the semi-final of the Yorkshire Cup. Going into the final moments of the game and with Halifax leading 5-0, Halifax's Mick Blacker came away with the ball and was challenged by Jonn Wolford on the half-way line. Now I had not only coached John at Bramley and at Odsal, but had studied his play for years and I knew that he was at his most dangerous when you least expected it, such as in this situation. I called out, unheard above the big crowd's shouts: "Don't pass Mick, hold the ball". Mick passed and John intercepted, ran to our full-back, Jimmy Birts, and sent the Dewsbury wingman striding for our line, to seemingly draw the game and take the replay back to Crown Flatt. But for some inexplicable reason the wingman crossed our line and put the ball down immediately instead of going under the posts. The conversion failed and we went on to play Leeds in the final. But that was 'Woolly', unpredictable and brilliant with it.

He went into coaching as joint coach at Hunslet alongside, you guessed it, Jack Austin, after he finally hung up his boots. John was Bramley's key player for possibly too many seasons, because an earlier change of club would surely have brought international status to this superb player who proved to the sceptics that he was big enough, heroically so.

	App	Tries	Goals	Pts
Bramley	406+4	79	23	283
Bradford Northern	93+5	16	9	57
Dewsbury	57+3	13	4	43
Hunslet	101+12	20	3	69
Yorkshire	1	0	0	0

Selections

It is every coach's wish to be able to select his 'dream team' a team from different eras, playing under the rules of their day. Let me begin by selecting my dream team from my younger days, before Super League, before the 10-yard onside at the play-the-ball, when scrums were competitive, and the tackling a tad higher and tougher. I will only go back to when I can remember those players with clarity and when I was at an age at which I could decide for myself if I rated a player rather than with an outside influence telling me I should.

Full-back: Martin Ryan (Wigan)
The first genuine 'running' full-back, who would look to run at the opposition instead of kick the ball or simply pass it on to a team mate. Ryan would also run into a third centre position from a winning scrum and make an overlap for the wingmen. He was originally a stand-off half so being able to evade tackles and make play for runners outside him came as second nature. He was a revelation when first introduced to this position and encouraged to open up the game from deep positions. A sound tackler, having the pace to put an opponent where he wanted him, his technique was of copybook standard. He won four Great Britain caps, took part in two Lions tours and made several Lancashire county appearances.

Right wing: Billy Boston (Wigan, Blackpool Borough)
A match winner in any company and at any time, Boston was big, fast and strong and possessed superb evasive qualities. His ability to score long-distance tries was an added bonus and he had the perfect understanding with his regular club and international centre partner, Eric Ashton. Using the natural power of such a big man, he was extremely dangerous near the opponents' try line as well as from deep and he scored many tries from scrums close to the opposition line, taking the pass directly from the scrum-half as he came infield from the wing position. A devastating 'crash' tackler, again coming in from the wing to smother the opposing centre, man-and-ball and thus preventing him from passing to his wing partner, Boston was a danger to all defences. He won 31 Great Britain caps and made two Lions tours. He scored an astounding 571 tries.

Right centre: Eric Ashton (Wigan)
The ideal centre threequarter, tall, pacy and with a strength that belied his slim build, Ashton was a St Helens lad who committed the cardinal sin of playing for Wigan. He captained Wigan to six Wembley finals, winning three, and was joined in all those finals by Billy Boston and ace forward, Brian McTigue. Eric captained Great Britain, both at home and on the 1962 Lions tour. After he retired from playing he went into coaching and

succeeded in coaching the 'big three' of Great Britain, Wigan and Leeds, before joining his home-town club, St Helens, on their board of directors. He won 26 caps for Great Britain and made two Lions tours, one as captain. He also scored 319 tries.

Left centre: Neil Fox (Wakefield Trinity, Bradford Northern, Hull KR, York, Bramley, Huddersfield)
Neil was big and strong - a magnificent player. Built like a second-row forward, he was also a superb left-footed goalkicker. A prolific points scorer, he kicked 1,955 goals and crossed the line for 316 tries in a career covering 536 games for Trinity alone and 628 in total. This total includes 17 appearances for Yorkshire, one for England, one for Great Britain versus The Rest and he also played for a Rugby League XIII. More importantly, Neil gained 29 Great Britain caps.

Left wing: Mick Sullivan (Huddersfield, Wigan, St Helens, York, Dewsbury)
Mick was possibly the toughest wingman to play for Great Britain. His devastating tackling was legend, his strength of mind and body was feared by opponents, and his football ability was of high international quality. He played wing, centre and scrum-half for his country in test football and is the joint record holder of Great Britain caps with 46. A teenager when making his international debut for the 1954 World Cup-winning Great Britain side in France, Sullivan went on two Lions tours, 1958 and 1962 and his career total of tries was 342.

Stand-off: Willie Davies (Bradford Northern)
With the back line listed above, a playmaker is required to give them the ball. Willie Davies was a magnificent stand-off, who could create openings or score himself. A master tactician, Willie was the outstanding number six of his era. He would bring not only a good measure of organisation but a vast amount of flair by which the star backs outside him would have a field day. His massive presence, alongside Ernest Ward and Jack Kitching at Bradford Northern, was one of the reasons for their dominance of the league at that time. Willie gained only three Great Britain test caps, but his era was full of classic stand-offs and the international caps were shared out in those days. Willie's battles with Ces Mountford, Dickie Williams, Willie Horne and Russ Pepperell were legend. He was on the Lions tour in 1946.

Scrum-half: Alex Murphy (St Helens, Leigh, Warrington)
Alex is arguably the best half-back Great Britain has ever produced. Jonty Parkin may challenge this claim, but Murphy's confidence in himself, verging on arrogance, would carry the day for this larger-than-life character from the Thatto Heath area of St Helens. He had skill in abundance, his self-confidence knew no bounds, and he had pace to burn, plus the strength to go with it. You could play him anywhere and he would come up trumps, play him where he wanted to play and you could

beat the world. He was a match-winner in any company and had that necessary commodity known as 'edge'. He thought he was the best in the world, and he played as if he was. Already a successful coach of international ability when he retired as a player, Alex accumulated 27 Great Britain caps, several for England and Lancashire and he holds the record as a coach for Wembley appearances with six to his credit. He won the Lance Todd Trophy in 1971 while playing for Leigh in their win over Leeds. Alex was a Lion on the 1958 and 1962 tours and was selected for a third trip in 1966 but missed out because of injury.

Prop: Terry Clawson (Featherstone Rovers, Hull KR, Leeds, Oldham)
One of many excellent prop forwards to chose from, Terry was a tough man, who was a very good footballer with a clever brain and great skills. I have chosen Terry mainly because of the respect he is held in by players who worked with him. His record in club and international football is excellent and his leadership first class. He was also a first-rate goalkicker and a very good man to have around in a tough match. Terry played 14 times for Great Britain and was a touring Lion in 1974.

Hooker: Tommy Harris (Hull FC)
The most capped Great Britain hooker with 25 caps, Tommy was a key man in the famous Hull FC pack that ruled the roost in the mid-1950s. A proud Welshman, Tommy was a Lions tourist in 1954 and 1958. A strong man, short in height but immensely powerful and an excellent dummy-half, he represented Wales on seven occasions and for my team, just shaded Joe Egan for the number nine shirt because he adds that extra bit of pace to the pack. He was Lance Todd winner in 1960 for Hull FC against Wakefield Trinity, despite his team losing 38-5.

Prop: Brian McTigue (Wigan)
For me Brian is the king-pin utility forward. Possessing great strength and toughness, Brian was also a wonderful passer of the ball, particularly in tight situations, with tacklers trying to knocking him over. A tower of strength in defence, he was the leading 'big hitter' in the various fearsome packs in which he played at Wigan. A terrific competitor who would not be beaten, Brian's ability was shown on his two Lions tours of 1958 and 1962, when of the 10 tests on those two tours, he played in nine of them, operating at both open and blind-side prop. His appearances for Lancashire were topped up with 25 Great Britain caps. He was a wonderful player.

Second-row: John Whiteley (Hull FC)
He was 'Gentleman' John Whiteley on and off the field. Make no mistake, being a gentleman did not diminish his toughness or the hard determination that produced this outstanding back-row forward. Big, fast and skilful, John made the 1957 World Cup side to Australia to become a Lion and again in 1958 on the full Lions tour. A classy, footballing forward

with pace and evasive qualities, John made 15 Great Britain appearances and also many for the Yorkshire team and on retiring as a player, coached at the highest level with great success, including the kudos of coaching the last Lions to win the Ashes on the 1970 tour. A tremendously cultured player John, along with Tommy Harris, formed one third of the outstanding Hull FC pack in his era.

Second-row: Dick Huddart (Whitehaven, St Helens, St George)
The first genuine wide forward runner; Dick used this power to blast his way through the tightest of defences. Making his name as a second rower at Whitehaven, he was transferred to Saints after his success on the 1958 Lions tour and made the trip again in 1962. Later he was transferred to the St George club in Sydney and played the remainder of his football in Australia. He gained 16 Great Britain caps, several for Cumberland and was the most exciting running forward ever to play in Britain. He won the Lance Todd Trophy in 1961 for Saints against Wigan and was certainly worth paying money to watch.

Loose-forward: Vince Karalius (St Helens, Widnes)
Again, any one of five or six were challenging for this vital last place in the pack. But Vinty took it by a whisker and on his only tour, in 1958, where the Australians nicknamed him 'the Wild Bull of the Pampas', earned his place in the folklore of our game. A mighty tackler and a big, roughhouse player with all the handling skills in the world to support his shock-trooper style, Vince is one of those brilliant loose-forwards we had then. His 10 caps for Lancashire added to his 12 for Great Britain were just reward for his sterling work during his super career.

Substitutes:

Lewis Jones (Leeds)
Lewis was a superlative footballer. Anyone who saw him play regularly would say: 'He was one of the best ever', and I agree. He was naturally skilful, fast, with a wonderful eye for an opening, an excellent kicking game, and evasive qualities which made him worth watching. His ability to play in almost every back position cries out for him to be a substitute in my team. A Welsh rugby union international, his 15 Great Britain caps on top of his Lions tour of 1954 make him a top-class utility back.

Derek Turner (Hull KR, Oldham, Wakefield Trinity)
There was not a loose-forward better than Derek Turner. If any change had to be made in my pack, in any position, I would put Derek into that spot with impunity. I would be ready to interchange Turner for Karalius after 15 minutes, then vice-versa, until the opposing team surrendered. A world-stage player, Derek won 24 Great Britain caps, one for England and nine for his county. Come to think of it, the first one into the dressing room, between Vince Karalius and Derek, could wear the number 13, it is

as close as that, but what substitutes both of them would make. Derek also went on to a brilliant coaching career after retiring as a player.

Cliff Watson (St Helens, Cronulla/Sutherland)
Thirty international caps, loads of medals for Wembley finals, Lancashire Cup finals etc, two tours as a Lion and a reputation second to none as a hard forward, plus the strength and determination to play anywhere in the pack makes Cliff the ideal interchange player. A wonderful capture from Midlands rugby union, he finished off his career in Australia and took some scalps there too. He would be a coach's dream today.

Dennis Hartley (Doncaster, Hunslet, Castleford)
'Big D' was a late starter to the game, but came on in leaps and bounds after his move to Parkside. As strong as a bull, his power on the run made him very dangerous near his opponent's line. With the experience of 11 test caps, several for his county and three Wembley finals, plus his Lions tour with the last successful Ashes winning British team of 1970, Dennis would be invaluable as an interchange player.

So there it is: my favourite players. What memories, what characters, what great blokes. As a final shot, I will submit, for your perusal, the best overseas side made up from players I coached over the years. See what you think.

Tony Currie (Australia), Neil Hunt (Australia), Andrew Ettingshausen (Australia), Dean Bell (New Zealand), Eric Grothe (Australia), Peter Jackson (Australia), Steve Martin (Australia), Peter Tunks (Australia), Trevor Clarke (New Zealand), Wally Fullerton-Smith (Australia), Sonny Whakarau (New Zealand), Trevor Paterson (Australia), Mark Laurie (Australia).

Substitutes: Marty Gurr (Australia), Terry Webb (Australia), Mark McGaw (Australia), Danny Campbell (New Zealand).

There are quite a few more I could pick but it would be an embarrassment to put any of my former players to find themselves in a second selection, safe to say they all figured in my selection process. I sincerely hope you enjoyed the read, it is hoped that it may stimulate your memory and you may say: "Oh yes, I remember him, but I think so-and-so was better'. That is what makes our game so special too: we may know some of the players I have mentioned personally, and our sport brings the supporter much nearer to the player than say soccer. Our superstars are still just ordinary guys who nod and say "Hi" when you meet them in the street. That's how it should be, that's what makes our game tick.

Thanks again for travelling with me through the superb game of rugby league football. It's great.

148